PAUL
MESSENGER OF GRACE

PAUL
MESSENGER OF GRACE

KENNETH SCHENCK

wesleyan
publishing
house

Indianapolis, Indiana

Copyright © 2010 by Kenneth Schenck
Published by Wesleyan Publishing House
Indianapolis, Indiana 46250
Printed in the United States of America
ISBN: 978-0-89827-439-4

Library of Congress Cataloging-in-Publication Data

Schenck, Kenneth, 1966-
Paul : messenger of grace / Kenneth Schenck.
    p. cm.
Includes bibliographical references.
ISBN 978-0-89827-439-4
1. Paul, the Apostle, Saint. I. Title.

BS2506.3.S34 2010
225.9'2--dc22

                                    2010029418

To Jimmy Dunn and Krister Stendahl

CONTENTS

PREFACE

This book and its sequel (*Paul—Soldier of Peace*) mean to present and reflect on the life and ministry of the apostle Paul by bringing the best of current scholarship into dialog with the concerns of Christian life. A good deal has taken place in the study of Paul these last thirty years, and not all of it has made its way from scholars to the pew. Some voices have expressed alarm at new perspectives on Paul, although for many of us in the Wesleyan tradition, these new perspectives fit very well with things we have always believed. Indeed, in some respects, those who most object to some of the new perspectives on Paul are the same individuals who have generally looked down on the thinking of the Wesleyan tradition.

For example, more than ever before, Pauline scholars recognize the importance of works in the Christian life. Perhaps the most decisive figure in the revolution in the study of Paul was E. P. Sanders, who surveyed all of the Jewish literature of Palestine and concluded that Jews kept the Law to stay in the covenant, not to get in. The Jewish emphasis on the Law was in response to God's grace, not an attempt to earn their salvation. This suggestion fits very well with the Wesleyan notion that we are not saved by works, but we must live a godly life through the power of the Spirit to stay in the faith.

I am dedicating each book in this series to two scholars who have revolutionized my understanding of Paul. I am dedicating this first volume to Krister Stendahl (1921–2008) and Jimmy Dunn. I never met Krister Stendahl, but his article, "Paul and the Introspective Conscience of the West," did more to transform my understanding of Paul than any other single source. His observations now seem so commonsensical, so obvious. Paul was a Jew and would not have seen his faith in Christ as a conversion from one religion to another, from Judaism to Christianity. Although Stendahl was a Lutheran bishop, his explanations of Romans 7 and Philippians 3 are thoroughly compatible with a Wesleyan perspective. Romans 7 is not Paul's current experience, nor is Paul leaving behind his sinful failures in Philippians 3 as he presses forward. Rather, Paul had a robust conscience, a strong sense of his blamelessness as a believer.

Jimmy Dunn is my Doctor Father, the brilliant mind under which I studied for my doctorate in New Testament. Not only is Professor Dunn a model scholar, a paragon of contextual interpretive method, but he is a Methodist lay pastor. While I was doing my doctoral studies in Durham, England, Professor Dunn wrote commentaries on 1 Corinthians and Colossians, and some of the insights of this current volume on 1 Corinthians come from the weekly New Testament seminar sessions where Dunn was working through that letter of Paul. For me, Dunn's greatest new perspective insight is that works of the Law in Paul are not so much good works in general but aspects of the Jewish Law that separated Jew and Gentile. Paul was not anti-works, but he was opposed to Jewish individuals who thought they had an advantage before God in salvation simply because they were circumcised.

Both volumes in this series have ten chapters, which are meant to follow roughly the chronological order in which Paul might have written these letters. Paul did not write his letters in the order they appear in the New Testament. Rather, his New Testament letters appear from longest (Romans) to shortest (Philemon). It is not possible to know which letters came first. Indeed, we cannot even be sure that Paul wrote 1 Thessalonians before 2 Thessalonians. The order I am treating these books is thus somewhat speculative—scholars regularly disagree on such things.

This book covers Paul's early years and conversion to faith in Christ. Then it looks at 1 Thessalonians, 1 Corinthians, Galatians, Philippians, and 2 Corinthians. The goal is not only to study these letters in their original settings in Paul's ministry, but also to reflect on them as Christian believers. How do we as Christians appropriate Paul's inspired words to these ancient audiences in our current contexts? In most chapters of these volumes, the first part of the chapter looks at the original message of a letter, while the second half reflects on the implications for our lives today. In the case of 1 Corinthians, the material is divided into multiple chapters.

Both volumes cover the general spectrum of Paul's teaching, even though they cover different letters. For example, while almost half of the second volume looks at various aspects of Romans, this volume covers Galatians, where we also find Paul wrestling with similar issues. While we look at the second coming by way of 1 Thessalonians in this volume, we look at similar issues in the second volume by way of 2 Thessalonians. In this way, readers can start with either volume and still get a good overview of Paul's thinking.

The target audience for this series is not the scholar but the pastor or layperson who wants to dig deeper into the original meaning of

Paul's letters and reflect more deeply on the intersection of those writings with Christian life today. We all bring a host of assumptions to our reading of Scripture, most of which probably serve us well as believers. But especially when we are so familiar with something, it is always helpful to realize there are other ways to look at various passages that have never occurred to us. It may not change our minds, but it helps us gain clarity and perspective on what we think.

I would like to thank those at Wesleyan Publishing House for the opportunity to write books of this sort. I am excited to see how God might use these two volumes and the Bible studies that are companion pieces. Wesleyan Publishing House gave me permission to blog through my first draft, and I am deeply appreciative to those who dialoged and debated with me over some of the ideas. At some points, they even changed my mind (particularly my ever-present interlocutor over Galatians, Richard Fellows).

Thanks also to those who have endured my classes on Paul at Indiana Wesleyan University over the years. The faculty of the School of Theology of Ministry also, and the newly formed Wesley Seminary at Indiana Wesleyan University, are some of the best people with whom one could work, and they also have heard their share of Paul from me over the years.

Lastly, my family regularly observes that I seem unable to detach myself from my laptop. To my wife Angie, step-daughters Stefanie and Stacy, and to Thomas and Sophia, my thanks for not leaving me to my own world but for constantly reminding me that there are other things that must be done like sledding and rescuing cats from garages. Thanks to God for such rich blessings in life as I enjoy.

March 15, 2010

BORN AT A TIME
AND PLACE

It's hard to understand what makes a person tick if you know nothing about his or her past. It would be enlightening to take Paul out for coffee and ask him a few things, to fill in a few blanks. Thankfully, he at least left three key passages where he gives us some personal information: Philippians 3:4–6; 2 Corinthians 11:21—12:10; and Galatians 1:13—2:14.

PAUL'S SELF-IDENTITY

We learn right away that Paul was a Jew.

One substantial difference between Paul's world and ours is the amount of significance we attach to the groups to which we belong. On a continuum with "individualist" on one end and "collectivist" on the other, modern, Western culture leans heavily toward the "individualist" end of the spectrum. Our identity is based much more on how we are different from other people than how we are like them. It was not so in Paul's world, where people's identity was focused on the groups they were in rather than who they were individually.

Identity in the ancient Mediterranean world was based primarily on three things: gender, geography, and genealogy.[1] Were you male or female (gender)? Where were you born, and what was your ethnicity (geography)? What was your family name, and what was its social status (genealogy)? We question these sorts of stereotypes and pigeonholes today, and, rightly so because they are the stuff of prejudice, and the more that gospel principles work themselves into the fabric of a community or society, the more its members will abandon the use of such labels to categorize one another.

If Western cultures tend to focus on the individual, sometimes too much, ancient and third-world cultures have tended to focus on the group or community. For example, marriages are often prearranged in group cultures, sometimes even before the children are born. This makes sense when identity is based on external features like gender, family, and race; you can know whether two people are compatible at, or even before, birth. Two families of the same race and similar background will pair up their children without considering their children's input or approval.

Today, we have such highly developed individual tastes and desires that we want to date to see if we are compatible. Will this other person make me happy? Will he or she irritate me by not squeezing the toothpaste from the bottom of the tube or by placing the toilet paper the wrong way on the roll? Most ancients spent their energies just trying to survive. They did not have the luxury and opportunity to worry about such trivial things.

PAUL THE JEW

So, Paul was a Jew. This was a significant statement of identity in his world. For an outsider, it meant, at the very least, he was strange. "Why don't you eat pork?" a Roman emperor once asked to a Jew who had waited months to see him about matters of life and death.[2] Jews were the ones who cut off the foreskins of their male children. And they did not work from sundown on Friday to sundown on Saturday, the day they called the Sabbath. These customs looked exceedingly strange to non-Jews.

For Paul growing up, though, it meant that he was a part of God's chosen people. He was a member of the nation God had chosen out of all the nations of the earth to walk with and bless, if Israel would only keep his commandments (see Deut. 32:8–9; 7:6–11). Paul was part of the nation to whom God had entrusted the "oracles of God," the Scriptures (Rom. 3:2 ESV). It was to Israel God had given all the promises that were being fulfilled in Christ (Rom. 9:4).

Since the early 100s, Christians have often had a skewed perspective on the Jews. We likely deserve some blame in various persecutions of Jews that have taken place over the centuries. Some of Martin Luther's comments on Jews in his later writings were atrocious, and thus, it is not too surprising that the Holocaust took place in Germany with significant support from many in the Lutheran and Roman Catholic churches of his country.[3]

It would be equally wrong—indeed the same sin—to paint all the Germans at that time as anti-Semitic. Germans like Dietrich Bonhoeffer and Rudolf Bultmann did not support Hitler. Bonhoeffer famously lost his life within months of the liberation of his prison for his opposition to Hitler. We will address some of the misconceptions of Judaism that still persist today in the next chapter.

PAUL THE GREEK

Paul called himself a "Hebrew of Hebrews" (Phil. 3:5; see also 2 Cor. 11:22) although he was not born in Jerusalem or to some well-established family of important Jews. He was born in Tarsus, in Asia

Minor (Acts 22:3).[4] His claim to be a Hebrew of the Hebrews meant that Aramaic was his first language and that his family was oriented around Aramaic-speaking Jerusalem. Yet, all his letters were written in fluent Greek. He quoted as much from the Greek translation of the Old Testament, the Septuagint, as he did the original Hebrew.

In short, he had all the makings of someone whom others might look down on as a diaspora Jew (a Jew who lived outside Israel; they were often suspected of compromising their faith to fit in with their culture). Someone might stereotype him as a Hellenistic Jew who spoke Greek instead of the Aramaic of the motherland. "No!" he might have protested in the days before he believed, "I am an Aramaic speaker like anyone in Jerusalem. In fact, I know Hebrew and read the Bible in the original language like the Pharisee and purist I am."

Whether this background accounts for some of Paul's zeal, we do not know. Did he spend his early life trying to prove himself to those who looked down on him or dismissed him because of where he was born? If so, he would not be the first or the last to do so.

PAUL THE ROMAN

This may be one reason Paul never mentioned anywhere in his writings that he was a Roman citizen, an honor very few in his world enjoyed. Was he ashamed of it? Was not Rome the political power that held sway over Jerusalem and the land of Israel? Would not the restoration of the land of Israel mean that the Messiah would overcome the hold of Rome?

Paul did not bring up his citizenship until Philippi, after he had suffered a beating and spent a night in jail (Acts 16:37). Perhaps he finally saw that he could use his citizenship to his advantage in spreading the gospel. At the very least, he could use it to get out of a few beatings!

If Paul was a Roman citizen from birth (see Acts 22:28), it suggests that his family had some status. Paul did not pay for his citizenship or receive it as a gift from someone important. His family already had this status before he was born. Perhaps his grandfather made tents for Julius Caesar when he was traipsing around the Mediterranean chasing Pompey. Or perhaps he made tents for Pompey. In any case, some important Roman seems to have rewarded one of Paul's ancestors with the great honor of Roman citizenship.

PAUL THE PHARISEE

It is possible that when Paul was back in Tarsus, he was the owner of a tent-making or leatherworking business rather than a menial laborer himself. At one point, he seemed to think of working with his hands as a kind of sacrifice for the sake of the gospel (1 Cor. 4:12). He had the means to travel and leave his hometown behind. At some point, he moved to Jerusalem, perhaps to live with his sister (Acts 23:16), and studied with the Pharisees.

Paul thus entered a different world than the one he was surrounded by as a child. He no longer learned Homer and how to separate Greek syllables. Now, he extended his knowledge of the Law, the Torah, and the traditions of the elders. What it meant to be a Pharisee will be addressed in the next chapter.

LIFE REFLECTIONS

We are all born at a particular place and time. We have no choice in the matter. In some parts of the world, particularly the West, we like to think we are free to be anything we want to be or do anything we want to do. But we had no choice regarding the circumstances surrounding our birth. Our most formative years are a kind of slavery to the contexts into which we are born. We are slaves to the forces at work on us, the genes we inherit from our parents, and the influences of our environment.

PRODUCTS OF OUR UPBRINGING

We cannot help whether we are born into poverty or wealth. We cannot help it if we are surrounded by peace or war. We cannot help it if we are raised in a Christian or Muslim family. Our most fundamental desires seem to be inherited from one place or another, long before we begin to reflect on whether we should have this set of desires or a different set.

As we grow up, we become freer to do the things we want, but most of us continue as slaves to the desires we inherited. We think of ourselves as free, but we mostly live out the desires and whims set in cement in our formative years. Education can help. We can learn about other ways of seeing things. Life can hold up a mirror and show us how others see us. When we truly see the other options, then we are freer to be or do something different from the enslavement of our childhood . . . or we can more freely choose to be what we already are.

But most of us seem content to live in ignorance of the forces at work in our lives. We assume the way we have learned to think is the only way to think. We have a built-in tendency to think those who act or think differently are either ignorant or evil. To the extent that we avoid self-reflection, we behave differently from the other animals around us, who are also influenced by the world around them.

FREEDOM OF THE WILL

Christians disagree over the extent to which God empowers us to choose him or not. Some believe God orchestrates everything in our lives so that we have no real choice whether to choose or not to choose him. The tradition I come from sees no way to reconcile this view of God with the fundamental affirmation that he is love. We believe that God, at some point in each person's life, offers a chance to move in his direction. The more we take that opportunity, the more power he gives us to keep moving toward him.

Paul was also born in a particular time and place. He was privileged to be born a Jew, which meant he was born with the Scriptures. In one sense, he started out on his journey to God farther along than those who were not born within Israel. Those of us who are born in a Christian context today start even farther along on that journey than where Paul started.

But Christians believe it is ultimately a personal journey, regardless of where we are born. If I am born into a devout Christian home, perhaps even baptized as a child, then I start out far along in the way. But my parents and church cannot go on the journey for me. I must move beyond the circumstances of my birth and become free in my choice of God.

PREVENIENT GRACE

What about those who have never heard? What of those who were born into a different set of religious beliefs? For example, it is hard to imagine a person born in fundamentalist Muslim circles believing in Christ, given his or her environment. Miracles, signs, and wonders have at times helped to convince people, but how many of these does the average individual in the world see in a lifetime?

Christian tradition long has had a sense that God will judge people according to the "light" they have. The Quakers used to speak of an inner light within everyone. Many Christians believe those who have never heard will be judged by how they responded to the light God gave them, not by whether they confess faith in a name they have never heard. Still others take the thought experiment further and suggest there may be anonymous Christians who have faith in God and are saved through Jesus even though they reject him with their conscious minds.

In the end, God is the one who decides eternal destinies. In one sense, it is foolish for any of us to think we know the answer to these questions. The righteous Judge will act justly; that we know for certain. We had best leave the rest to him.

John Wesley, the founder of Methodism, had a lovely concept we refer to today as prevenient grace, the grace of God that comes to us before we even can come to him. It can bring us to God in the most beautiful way if we allow it. Although it is God's business, I like to think that no matter who you are, no matter what the circumstances of your origins—your gender, geography, and genealogy—God will be there, drawing you to himself. It is not where we start that is important but where we end up.

REMOVING CULTURAL BARRIERS

The ancient world reminds us that identity is more than just a matter of me—what I want and what I like. At the same time, the basic principles of Christianity require us to move beyond the group mentality of the ancient world. The gospel says "there is neither Jew nor Greek, slave nor free, male nor female, for . . . all are one in Christ Jesus" (Gal. 3:28).

A person is not more valuable to God simply because he is a man or a Jew. Everyone is equally loved by God. One of the great insights of the modern world—one we are in danger of losing—is that you cannot assume a person is a certain way because she is a woman or a certain color or from a certain place. No one can argue today that all men are better leaders, more insightful, or even stronger than all women. If the gospel required us to believe such things, it would be false.

But the principles of the gospel require us to let each individual, regardless of gender, race, or social status, define his or her own identity, beliefs, and actions. Christianity is never an excuse for unloving behavior. Yet, some Christians use the Bible as an excuse to treat certain groups of people hatefully. Here we remember the words of Jesus to such people in Matthew 7:23, "I never knew you. Away from me, you evildoers!" (TNIV).

FOR FURTHER REFLECTION

1. To what extent have you been freed from the "enslavement" of where you were born? To what extent is how you think and act simply a function of forces at work in you rather than conscious decisions you made after reflection and study of other options? To what extent have you embraced Christ as your own, rather than riding on the decision of your parents or those around you?

2. Where would you say you fall on a spectrum between a person whose identity is almost completely a function of the groups to which you belong and a person who does your own thing no matter what? What steps would you need to take to become more balanced in your sense of identity?

3. To what extent would you say you live out the principle that, in Christ, wealth, status, power, gender, or race should make no difference in how much you value others or show love to others? What concrete steps can you take to move closer to God's will in this area?

2

A CHANGE IN
LIFE DIRECTION

As we learned in the first chapter, Paul was a Jew, a descendant of Abraham. He was from the tribe of Benjamin and a "Hebrew of Hebrews" (Phil. 3:5). By this expression, he meant to say not only that Aramaic was his first language, but that he was also raised on the values of purist Jerusalem society. These were the ones who thought they did Judaism the right way, not like those *diaspora* (Greek "scattered") Jews. Diaspora Jews usually spoke Greek or—even worse—whatever obscure local language the people used where they lived.[1]

PAUL'S KEEPING OF THE LAW

Before Paul believed, he belonged to a group called the Pharisees, and he followed their approach to keeping the Jewish Law (Phil. 3:5).[2]

Paul claimed to be blameless when it came to the kind of righteousness you could have in keeping the Jewish Law (3:6). Many of us seem to somehow miss this statement. Paul said he was "faultless" in the way he kept the Law, even before he believed in Christ.

If we can get beyond what we have heard about Paul to what he actually said, we will gain a lot of insight. If we listen to what Paul said about himself, both before and after he believed, we will see that he did not consider himself a moral failure apart from Christ. Nor did he think of himself as a slave to sin after he followed Jesus.[3]

LOSS BECAUSE OF CHRIST

Paul did not present his past as a time of failure. Instead, he said that "whatever gains I had, these I have come to regard as loss because of Christ" (Phil. 3:7 NRSV). He called his Jewish badges of honor "gain," not illustrations of his past sinfulness or moral failure. Later, when he said, "forgetting what lies behind" (3:13 NRSV), he was not forgetting all his past failures. He said nothing of the sort. He forgot things that, from a certain human perspective, might have been quite impressive.

The problem was that these things simply were not (and are not) what God is looking for—no mere mortal could ever be good enough to earn God's favor. In the end, all such accomplishments pale next to the power of Christ's faithful death and resurrection—this is what God is looking for.

POWERLESS WITHOUT THE SPIRIT

Christians often take Romans 7:14–25 as an indication not only of Paul's past moral struggle, but also of a struggle he continued to have with sin as a Christian. Paul used the present tense when he said, "the evil I do not want is what I do" (7:19 NRSV). After all, do not so many of us Christians identify with Paul's alleged struggle with sin? Do we not find ourselves often struggling to do the right thing, even though on some level we truly want to?

But our identification with these words in our own lives does not determine what Paul meant two thousand years ago. The broader context of Romans 7 shows that these words were not about a current struggle in Paul's life. In Romans 6:17–18; 7:5–6; and 8:1–4, Paul urged that Christians were no longer slaves to sin, but slaves to righteousness. If Paul were talking of his current struggle, then he would be implying he himself was not truly a Christian!

The majority of Pauline scholars now acknowledge that in Romans 7:14–25, Paul was portraying those who wanted to do the good of the Jewish Law but were unable because they did not have the Holy Spirit to empower them. It is irrelevant that he was speaking in the present tense, since it is perfectly natural to use the present tense when you are playing out a hypothetical scenario. In the end, you would have to rip this chapter from its context to make of it what so many Christian readers try to do today. Paul was not talking about some current struggle or some inevitable struggle a believer cannot avoid.

BLAMELESS BEFORE THE LAW

Some scholars, while acknowledging that Paul was not talking about a current struggle, have suggested he was remembering a struggle from his past. All I can say is that Paul almost never gave that impression when he talked about his past. I find nothing of this tone in Philippians 3 or 2 Corinthians 11, for example. Words like *repentance* and *forgiveness* do not show up often in Paul's writings, as some fossil of former worries. From his earliest letters, he urged his readers to be blameless in their lives (see 1 Thess. 5:23; Phil. 1:10–11) and suggested they follow his example (see 1 Thess. 1:6–7; Phil. 3:17).[4]

The parable of the Pharisee and the tax collector is probably a good picture of what Paul was like before he believed in Christ (Luke 18:9–14).[5] It is easy to picture Paul saying in his former life, "God, I thank you that I am not like other people—robbers, evildoers, adulterers—and these lawless Christians." He exuded a similar confidence and authoritative tone toward his churches after he believed. Paul's phrase, "Hebrew born of Hebrews; as to the law, a Pharisee; as to zeal, a persecutor of the church; as to righteousness under the law, blameless" (Phil. 3:5–6 NRSV) has a similar tone to the comment of the Pharisee who says, "I fast twice a week; I give a tenth of all my income" (Luke 18:12 NRSV).

At the same time, we must not make blanket assumptions about Judaism or even about Pharisees in Jesus' day. The caricatures that work so well in popular preaching have also fed holocausts and crusades. We are now so used to Christianity and Judaism being separate religions that we forget the earliest Christians were Jews and probably identified themselves as Jews to their deaths. Paul spoke of Gentile believers being "grafted in" the tree whose "natural branches" remained ethnic Jews (see Rom. 11:17–21). He believed that, around the time of Christ's return, the bulk of non-believing Israel would also come to believe (Rom. 11:26).

There is a popular fiction sometimes heard in preaching, that Saul was Paul's Jewish name, and Paul was his Christian name. But a careful reading of Acts dispels this idea. The book of Acts continues to call him Saul some fifteen years into his life as a Christian, only suddenly to switch to Paul while he is on the island of Cyprus (Acts 13:9). The best explanation of Paul's dual names is that one of these is his nickname, and the other is part of his name as a Roman citizen.

AT THE FEET OF GAMALIEL

At some point in his early years, Paul became a Pharisee. Perhaps his family, even though living outside Israel, maintained some connection with Jerusalem. Perhaps Paul moved to Jerusalem to reconnect with that Hebrew of Hebrews part of his past. Whatever his motivation, Paul was instructed "at the feet of Gamaliel" (Acts 22:3 NRSV). Does this mean that Paul apprenticed as a Pharisee with Gamaliel? We know the Pharisees had two principal schools at this time: the schools of Hillel and Shammai. Jewish tradition says Gamaliel was the grandson of Hillel and thus a Hillelite.[6]

Gamaliel's speech to the Sanhedrin about their response to Christianity sounds very much like a Hillelite (Acts 5:34–39). The Shammaites seemed to have engaged more in political action; the Hillelites let things unfold as they would. Gamaliel argued fatalistically that the Sanhedrin did not need to take any action against the apostles because God would sort out the situation.[7]

Paul's approach in Acts was not like Gamaliel's, to say the least. Paul served the Sanhedrin in tracking down and arresting certain Christians, although the apostles themselves were apparently never the target of Paul's persecutions.[8] He seems mostly to have targeted Greek-speaking, Christian Jews like Stephen and Philip. Perhaps they were even more radical in their understanding of Christ than the Aramaic speaking believers in Jerusalem. So, for example, when the Hellenists were scattered in Acts 8, the apostles were able to stay put (Acts 8:1).

PHARISEE OF THE PHARISEES

It has been very convenient to stereotype the Pharisees as hypocritical legalists, and perhaps many were. This is certainly the dominant picture that we get from the gospel of Matthew. Matthew 23 is a major critique of Pharisees who did not practice what they preached. Matthew told his audience that the Jews should obey the Pharisees because they were the bearers of Moses's authority, but he criticized them for not following their own teaching (23:2–3).

At the same time, we should bear in mind that the other gospels are not as harsh or dismissive of the Pharisees, especially Luke-Acts (scholars are now nearly unanimous that Luke and Acts are two volumes of a single work). Some scholars think Matthew's gospel was written in the decade after the destruction of Jerusalem in A.D. 70, when the Pharisees were in power and hostile to Christianity. This could be the reason Matthew presented the Pharisees more negatively. By contrast, Acts speaks of Christian Pharisees (15:5) and calls Paul a Pharisee in the present tense (23:6). Thus Luke-Acts does not seem to view Pharisees as so diametrically opposed to believers as Matthew does.

The origin of the Pharisees is uncertain, although they clearly emerged in the mid-second century B.C. Some consider them the heirs of the *hasidim* or "faithful ones" of the Maccabean revolt, individuals who chose to die rather than battle on the Sabbath. Their name means "separated ones." Perhaps their goal was to keep the Jewish Law so well that God would restore Israel as a nation and then usher in a golden age because of their faithfulness.

We thus need to make a careful distinction between people who are very disciplined in their lifestyle and people who are legalists. Legalism is when you like rules simply because you like rules—rules for their own sake and often as more important than people. But someone might also live a strict life out of genuine devotion to God. We would be wrong to call such a person a legalist. Surely numerous Pharisees fell into this category, individuals like Nicodemus who lived a strict life out of true devotion to God.

It is hard to know what Paul's motivation as a Pharisee was in persecuting the early believers. Did he think that his zealous acts would help bring about the political restoration of Israel? Was he psychologically battling the stereotype of someone from the diaspora, trying to prove he was not some kind of liberal or lightweight Greek-speaking

Jew? What was it about the Hellenistic believers in particular that he found so threatening?

The answers are not known for sure.

LIFE REFLECTIONS

The story of Paul's conversion to Christianity in Acts is often used as a model for how to come to Christ, for how one becomes a Christian.[9]

CONVERSION

One recent book by Richard Peace presents Paul as a model of (1) gaining insight into your true state and who Jesus truly is, (2) turning toward Christ, and (3) transformation.[10] No doubt many individuals, particularly those with a more traditional mindset, resonate with this standard model of getting saved. You recognize your need for Christ, repent of your sins, acknowledge and surrender to him as Lord, and then the Holy Spirit transforms you and makes you a new creation. However, part of Peace's goal is to show that for many people, their awareness of and turning to Christ is a process that takes place more gradually.

Repentance is not a popular theme today, not when it is properly understood as a real, substantial recognition of what is wrong in your life and the need for a change in your life direction. Ironically, never in history have Christians so easily confessed themselves as sinners, and never in history have they been so comfortable with it! True insight into Christ and true repentance entails a passionate desire to change, and in that sense, it is worth considering whether many who call themselves Christians today are even converted.

ETERNAL DESTINY

The question of eternal destiny is a distinct question from conversion. Whom will God rescue from the most definitive judgment yet to come? Many traditions, including my own, have tended to believe that God will judge each person "according to the light they have." Certainly, Christians have historically believed that Christ is the only path by which someone can be saved. But does God sometimes save individuals through Christ even though they have never heard of him? Does God weigh each of us according to the insight we have? My own tradition has tended to answer this question in the affirmative.

In addition, many of those who grow up in fervent Christian homes do not have as radical a turning as Paul did. There are surely people who would have escaped God's judgment at every point in their lives. When they were children, they did not know about Christ and God would have accepted them. Then the first time they recognized the lordship of Christ, they surrendered to him as King. They have served Christ ever since. Such individuals have been saved at every point of their life and have never undergone a radical turning.

THE HOLY SPIRIT

For Paul, the key moment when one became Christ's was neither when he gained insight nor when he turned to him, but when he received the Holy Spirit. This was when God put "his seal of ownership" on him (see 2 Cor. 1:21–22). The lead up to insight or repentance may take various lengths of time for different people. But the Spirit is the key ingredient to being a Christian. It is not that God is prohibited from showing mercy on individuals who have not come to this point, but Paul seemed to have drawn a fairly clear line between out and in.

When does this event happen? For some, it is a dramatic experience, as Acts depicts Paul's entrance into salvation (9:1–19). For others, it may be a dawning realization of something that has already happened somewhere along the way. Luke says that John the Baptist was filled with the Spirit even in the womb (Luke 1:15), so we cannot deny that some children have had the Holy Spirit long before they had the insight to confess faith.

So, the conversion of Paul in Acts may resonate with some, particularly those for whom coming to Christ involved a radical turning from one way of life to another or from one understanding to another. Others may resonate with the model of a long process of turning to Christ.[11] Still others, particularly those from traditions that baptize their children, may resonate more with John the Baptist's experience, a man who grew up following God's leading from his earliest days.

FOR FURTHER REFLECTION

1. Take a moment to read Romans 6:17–18; 7:5–6; and 8:1–4, which form the context for Romans 7:14–25. To what extent do you agree with the claim that the surrounding context makes it very unlikely that Paul was speaking of his current experience in 7:14–25? How new to you is the idea that Paul was not a person who felt much like a moral failure, either before or after he came to Christ? If you adopted this perspective, how would it change how you view sin in your own life?

2. What do you think about the claim that Judaism and Christianity were not distinct religions in the New Testament as they are today? How would it change the way you read the New Testament to think of Peter and Paul as Christian Jews even more than as Jewish Christians?

3. To what extent would you say you have used stereotypes of the Pharisees to justify your attitudes toward those around you today? Have you ever had a legalistic attitude toward others, or have you ever dismissed someone as a legalist? Evaluate your attitude given the distinction in this chapter between being strict and being a legalist. Is God leading you to change your attitude?

4. Can you identify a point in your life where you received the Holy Spirit or when you became a Christian? Was it a decision you made at a point in time, or was it a long process leading to a moment of recognition? What do you think makes the difference between someone who will be saved when Christ returns and someone who will not? To what extent do you agree or disagree with the idea that God will judge us all according to how we have responded to the light we have?

3

THE UNKNOWN YEARS

Paul's writings say little of the time between his conversion and when he started to write letters to churches he founded. It is true there are several chapters in Acts (chapters 13–18) about this period. But from a historical standpoint, we should be careful. When Luke's outline of Jesus' life is compared to Matthew's, Mark's, and John's, there are differences both in the order of events and the writer's perspective on certain events. We might expect the same to be true if the other gospel writers had written about Paul's life, each from his own perspective. So, we have to remember that we're left with only one perspective on these events in Paul's life, rather than the four we have in the Gospels. If we had additional perspectives, we might come away with a slightly different impression of what happened than what seems obvious to us from Acts.

The reason for the different perspectives is that the writers of the gospels and Acts were doing more than simply presenting history. They argued for certain points of view, and the manner of their presentation serves that purpose and not the modern quest to present historical data as objectively as possible.[1] However, since the Acts account and Paul's comments in his letters are all the record we have, while heeding the warning, we must examine these sources if we want to flesh out these years.

AFTER HIS CONVERSION

Starting with Paul's comments, we can at least sketch a basic framework of his activities in the lost years. In Galatians 1:16–18, Paul said he did not go up to Jerusalem after God revealed himself to him. Instead, he went to a place he called Arabia. Then he returned to Damascus, and finally, three years after the first revelation, went up to Jerusalem for a brief period of about two weeks. He went there to see Peter (whom he calls by his Aramaic name, Cephas). He also met James, the brother of Jesus (Gal. 1:19). He wrote that he did not see any of the other apostles on that visit.

Paul's comments can give us a glimpse at what another version of Acts might look like if one had been written. Most of what Paul wrote fits with the account in Acts 9. But Paul and Acts give us slightly different impressions of what happened. For example, Acts 9:19 says Paul spent "several days," even "many days" (9:23) with the disciples in Damascus. But without Paul's comment in Galatians, we probably would not interpret those statements to mean three years.

The difference in impression is even greater when it comes to Paul's brief stay in Jerusalem. Galatians 1:18 says it was fifteen days and that Paul only met Peter and James. But Acts says Paul moved freely throughout Jerusalem and preached boldly (9:28). More to the point, Acts says Barnabas took the initiative to introduce Paul to the apostles (9:27). So, the impression from Paul is that he had a brief, private meeting with

Peter and James. Acts gives the impression that Paul met the entire leadership of the Jerusalem church and then only left Jerusalem because certain Greek-speaking Jews were after him (9:29–30).

Arabia in Paul's World

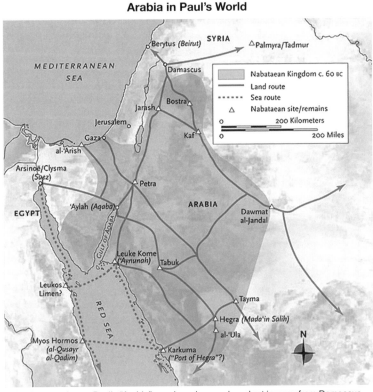

As the map shows, Paul's "Arabia" may have been only a short journey from Damascus.

What Paul meant by "Arabia" in Galatians 1:17 is open for debate. Some have thought Paul actually travelled to the Sinai Peninsula where the Law was first revealed (see Gal. 4:25). However, the logistics of travel to Damascus, north of Galilee, make it likely that Paul's Arabia was the Nabatean kingdom, just to the east of Damascus. Petra, the leading city of that kingdom, was where King Aretas IV ruled, the king whose Arab governor tried to arrest Paul outside Damascus (see 2 Cor. 11:32).

The difference between Paul's own account of his escape and the Acts account gives us a glimpse into Luke's approach to telling the early Christian story. Acts 9 tells us that "the Jews" of the city tried to kill Paul (9:23) because they did not like his preaching. But Paul said that the representative of the Arabian king Aretas was trying to arrest him (2 Cor. 11:32), presumably because of something he had done when he had visited Arabia.

We often picture Paul praying and studying during these first three years as a believer, going to seminary, as it were, to sort out the cognitive dissonance of his conversion. But it seems very likely he almost immediately recognized God's call on him as an apostle and started to preach to those in Arabia (see Gal. 1:16). Perhaps his earliest preaching was rather confrontational.[2] It is possible that Paul's earliest preaching adopted whatever slightly more radical version of the gospel Stephen and the Greek-speaking believers had preached, a message that caused Stephen to be stoned. Paul soon found himself treading rough waters in his earliest days.

Maybe the Jews of Damascus and the ethnic leader of the Arabs in the city were out to get him. But if we had to choose which problem was bigger, it's helpful to know that Acts consistently downplayed opposition to Paul from secular authorities and instead emphasized the Jews as his opponents. For Luke, this recurring theme was probably a tacit explanation for why God allowed the Romans to destroy Jerusalem. Unfortunately, Christians in history have occasionally ripped this theme of mainstream Jewish rejection of Jesus from its historical and literary context and have made it an excuse for anti-Semitism and the persecution of Jews in our time. But if we truly want to understand how the gospel first unfolded, we must take Acts' tendencies into account in our reconstruction. Suffice it to say that Paul probably had a pretty good handle on who was creating problems for him.

The best guess for when Paul might have escaped Damascus puts him in the city around A.D. 36–37. This dating would put his coming to faith around A.D. 33–34, about three years after Jesus rose from the dead. Sometime around A.D. 36, Herod Antipas—the one who beheaded John the Baptist—was driven out of power in Damascus for a short time by King Aretas. It was a point in time when Arab power in the city was probably at a peak.

BACK TO TARSUS

Both Paul and Luke indicate that Paul returned to Asia Minor after his first visit to Jerusalem (Gal. 1:21; Acts 9:30). Acts says more specifically that it was Tarsus, and that Tarsus was Paul's home town. He stayed in that area until some ten years later, when Barnabas took the initiative to take Paul to Antioch (Acts 11:25–26). What was Paul doing all those years? It seems likely that he was spreading the good news throughout his home territories. His tussle with Aretas in Damascus shows that his ministry emerged before Barnabas arrived in Tarsus. Paul was probably preaching all these years, a good explanation for why he never spent time in his home region during his later missionary journeys.

Paul also alluded to a major spiritual experience he had during those years. In 2 Corinthians 12:1–4, Paul spoke of a man who was taken up into the third heaven. He was unsure whether it was an out of body experience or whether the man physically went to the highest heaven. It is clear he was talking about himself, since he went on to tell of how God let him have a "thorn in [the] flesh" so that he would not boast about such revelations (12:7). Paul said this experience happened "fourteen years ago" (v. 2), which would put it in the early A.D. 40s, while he was in and around Tarsus.[3]

Paul said in Galatians 2 that his next trip to Jerusalem was "after fourteen years" (2:1 NRSV). The most obvious way to take this comment is that Paul believed in Jesus (ca. A.D. 33), then went to Jerusalem for the first time some three years later (A.D. 36), and then went to Jerusalem a second time some fourteen years later (ca. A.D. 50). This is in fact how most scholars have reconstructed Paul's chronology, placing his second visit to Jerusalem around A.D. 49.[4]

However, this straightforward interpretation causes difficulties when compared with Acts. Here, you will have to decide for yourself how precise both Paul and Acts intend to be in their recounting of historical events. The tension is twofold. First, Acts 11:27–30 tells of a trip that Barnabas and Paul made to Jerusalem to take famine relief from Antioch. The best estimates are that this famine took place around the year A.D. 46, although the relief could have been taken earlier.

F. F. Bruce makes an ingenious suggestion on this point. He notes that the word for "after" in Galatians 2:1 can also be translated as "through." So, he wonders if "after fourteen years" (NRSV) actually started from Paul's conversion rather than from his previous trip.[5] Paul's second trip would then be around A.D. 46–47, during the famine. Further, Paul said in Galatians 2:2 that he went up to Jerusalem because of a revelation. Was it not a prophecy that led to the famine relief in Acts 11?

But this chronology creates another tension between Paul and Acts. Paul did not go to Jerusalem in Galatians 2 because of someone else's revelation about a famine. Paul went because of a revelation God gave specifically to him. In addition, the revelation was about the way he preached to the Gentiles, not about a famine. This is where Bruce's interpretation falls short. The topic of Paul's second visit to Jerusalem in Galatians 2 was not a famine, but actually much more similar to the Jerusalem Council described in Acts 15.

Most scholars have thus concluded that Galatians 2 and Acts 15 are two different versions of the same basic event. They involve the same people and cover the same issue—whether Gentile believers must get circumcised to be saved. The problem is that the two accounts each have their own flavor. Paul's visit in Galatians 2 was private, informal, and initiated by Paul. The so-called Jerusalem Council in Acts 15 was public, somewhat formal, and initiated by the church at Antioch.

Bruce suggests that Galatians 2 was about a private visit Paul made during the famine relief trip in Acts 11. Then Acts 15 was a more formal visit on the subject a couple years later, after Paul and Barnabas went on their first missionary journey. Bruce also argues that Galatians was written before the Jerusalem Council of Acts 15, another indication of the conflict over whether Gentiles needed to be circumcised to escape God's judgment.[6] You will have to draw your own conclusion. I have found it impossible to get past the "after fourteen years" (NRSV) of Galatians 2. Perhaps Paul was omitting reference to the gift trip of Acts as irrelevant to the topic at hand. You will have to decide how creative Luke allowed himself to be in his representation of the early church in Acts.

What is clear is that Paul did have some sort of showdown with other factions in the early church over whether or not and how Gentiles might escape God's coming judgment. Paul eventually came to the understanding that as long as Gentiles truly had faith in Jesus as their Lord, then they were children of God just as the Jews. Formally or informally, Paul secured agreement on the issue from the leaders of the Jerusalem church, especially Peter and James, Jesus' brother. They might not have said it the same way as Paul, but they affirmed that Gentiles could escape God's wrath without fully converting to Judaism and being circumcised.

Paul won this concession sometime around the year A.D. 49, when he took Titus to Jerusalem as an example of an uncircumcised man who had believed (Gal. 2:2–3). The Jerusalem leaders did not force him to become circumcised. However, the wording suggests that they still thought it preferable. Paul indicated there were other people involved who were putting pressure on the Jerusalem leaders. He called them "false brothers" (Gal. 2:4–5). Luke considered them Christians (Acts 15:5).

But the Jerusalem leadership had its limits. Paul did not fare as well in an incident that took place not long after this initial agreement. At Antioch, Peter was visiting and eating with Gentile believers—that is, until Jesus' brother, James, who had apparently become the leader of the church in Jerusalem, clamped down. Even Peter seems to have recognized James' authority over him. James convinced Peter—and Paul's missionary companion Barnabas—to stop eating with Gentile believers, presumably because they brought the potential threat of being unclean.

Acts 15 offers a verdict on the Jew-Gentile issue that seems to address this issue as well—the question of how Jew and Gentile can eat together. Bruce thinks the incident at Antioch and the writing of Galatians took place prior to the Jerusalem Council in Acts 15. Other scholars suggest that Acts 15 is meant to capture in one story a process that historically actually took a longer amount of time to develop and unfold.[7] Each reader will have to make up his or her own mind.

In either case, the Jerusalem leadership concluded that if Gentiles would follow certain purity guidelines, then the Jews could eat with them (see Acts 15:29). Eating together was of major importance for the early Christians. Jews saw table fellowship as a central element in belonging to God's people. You ate with those who were truly your people and in your family.

So, Gentiles would need to stay away from food that had come from a pagan temple and had been sacrificed initially to another god. Much of the meat in any ancient marketplace came from nearby pagan temples. Only the fat was burned in the sacrifice. In addition, Gentiles would need to kill any animals used for food by slitting the throat and draining the blood. Blood could not be a part of the meal in any way. Finally, the Gentiles themselves would need to abstain from sexual immorality, which would make them contagiously impure.

Paul agreed with the part about sexual immorality (see 1 Cor. 5:11). But he took a don't-ask-don't-tell approach to matters of food. "I know and am persuaded in the Lord Jesus that nothing is unclean in itself; but it is unclean for anyone who thinks it unclean" (Rom. 14:14 NRSV). It is thus no surprise that he never endorsed the position of the Jerusalem church on this issue in any of his writings, even when he dealt with these issues.

Bruce would like to see the Jerusalem Council solving all these issues and everyone going on in harmony.[8] Acts does not even mention this particular conflict, a fact that confirms a general tendency on its part to minimize early Christian disagreements.

However, it seems little coincidence that Paul and Barnabas had a falling out about this time, even though Acts tells us it focused on whether to take a young man named John Mark on a missionary journey (Acts 15:36–40). They went their separate ways. It seems Paul lost the argument at Antioch over table fellowship between Jew and Gentile. Paul never claimed he won the day in the Antioch argument, as he did in relation to his visit to Jerusalem and as his personality would lead us to expect from him. The best explanation is he probably did not convince the leadership of his position.

Paul thus embarked on his second missionary journey with Silas, at odds with the Jerusalem church. Although Acts gives a passing mention of a quick visit to Jerusalem in the mid-50s (Acts 18:22), Paul would not make another substantial visit to Jerusalem again until the time when he was arrested.[9]

PAUL'S FIRST AND SECOND MISSIONARY JOURNEYS

In the time between the famine in Jerusalem (ca. A.D. 46) and the Jerusalem Council (ca. A.D. 49), Paul embarked on what most call his first missionary journey. This journey started from Antioch with Paul, Barnabas, and John Mark, who was Barnabas's cousin (see Col. 4:10). The first stop was the island of Cyprus, which Acts tells us was Barnabas' home land. Acts also gives the impression that Barnabas was the leader of the missionary expedition.

Paul's First Missionary Journey

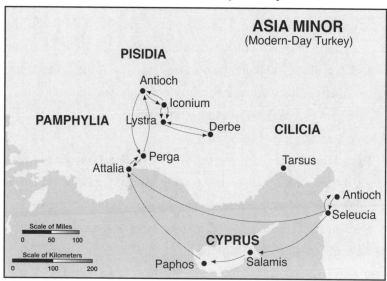

After the group finished preaching the gospel on Cyprus, they headed north for the mainland of Asia Minor, or modern-day Turkey. This region may not have been part of the original plan. The mountains became higher as they travelled inland, and Paul seemed increasingly to be exploring the possibility of bringing the gospel to the Gentiles. Perhaps he was also increasingly taking charge. We know

Paul had a way of getting into trouble with local authorities—they had already been brought before the Roman governor of Cyprus, although that encounter had turned out well.

For one or maybe all of these reasons, once the group reached Pamphylia, the southern part of Asia Minor, John Mark abandoned the group and returned to Jerusalem. According to Acts, this is the primary reason why Paul and Barnabas later parted ways. Paul considered John Mark unreliable as a traveling companion.

The rest of the trip involved the southern part of the Roman region known as Galatia. This included visits to towns like Antioch in Pisidia, Iconium, Lystra, and Derbe. Paul was stoned and left for dead at Lystra, but miraculously survived. Most scholars believe that this collection of cities and villages was the target audience of the New Testament book of Galatians, although the northern region was the favorite until the twentieth century. Acts only tells us of Paul founding churches in this southern part of Galatia, and the northern region is not on the way to anywhere we know Paul went.

Thus, some sixteen or seventeen years after Paul believed in Christ, he and a man named Silas embarked from Antioch on what is conventionally known as Paul's second missionary journey. In truth, he had been on a mission since he turned to Christ. He went on a mission to Arabia. He no doubt evangelized his home region of Cilicia for years. Then he went with Barnabas to south Galatia. By the time he embarked toward Greece, he had been proclaiming the gospel for almost twenty years.

LIFE REFLECTIONS

Paul's ministry, even in his earliest years, provides us so many lessons for life and the church it is hard to know where to begin. His initial turn to faith in Jesus as the Jewish messiah is a reminder never to lose hope that someone's life will be changed by the gospel. The person who seems most hardened, whom we could hardly imagine believing, might one day surprise us. It must have been hard for those early Christians to believe that Paul was truly a believer, and that his conversion was anything but a trick.

A RADICAL CHANGE

At the same time, look at what a radical change it was! Paul went from pursuer to the pursued, and he soon found himself with opponents among the Christians. He went from not going with the faith to going too far with the faith—at least in the minds of some Christians. In the same way, watch out for new converts who have so fully turned to Christ. Sometimes they change so radically that they make the rest of us uncomfortable.

The radical convert is not always right on everything. Did Paul have to do whatever he did to get himself in trouble with the Arab ethnarch (ethnic leader) in Damascus? Should Paul have accused Peter of hypocrisy in front of the whole church at Antioch (Gal. 2:14)? Maybe Barnabas's approach, attempting to find middle ground and a more conciliatory way, is sometimes more prudent or effective. But radical converts also have a way of showing us our own inconsistencies and complacency. If the goal is to be more Christlike, then we should welcome their observations and see if God is trying to speak to us through them.

A SPECIAL TASK

Paul was a person before he was a character in Scripture. Though he was a person of great influence, a significant figure, any Christian in the first century might have felt free to disagree with him. They did not know the Holy Spirit would steer his writings into Scripture, while leaving the champions of other perspectives strangely silent.

Paul seems to have been a fiery, demanding person. From what we see in the New Testament, he was an intelligent, passionate, forthright person. Sometimes his mouth got him into trouble. Different people have different personalities and different God-ordained goals. God does not want us all to take on the personality of Paul or even the tasks of Paul.

God did a special thing through him. Christianity seems to have grown significantly out of his ministry. Certainly a vibrant church grew in the East. We can question whether God has in store for any of us alive today as big a task as Paul's ministry would prove to be. Paul sometimes told his churches to imitate him (see 1 Cor. 4:16; Phil. 3:17), but he did not mean he wanted them to become full-blown apostles like him. Such was not in God's design for everyone. God had a special task for Paul, just as he has for us.

A DIVERSITY OF OPINION

Paul's relationship and disagreement with some of the Christians in the Jerusalem church is enlightening. Many people like to think of the early church as a time when everyone agreed and there were no denominations. Everyone was truly full of the Spirit and lived the ideal Christian life.

In reality, the early church was diverse, with groups that were so different from each other that we might almost call them denominations. Paul's own churches did not always recognize his authority, let alone the church headquarters back in Jerusalem. Peter and James probably would have preferred Gentile converts become circumcised and fully convert to Judaism. They chose not to compel Titus to be circumcised, which leads us to believe they might have preferred it (Gal. 2:3). They did not allow a Jewish believer to eat with a Gentile believer unless the Gentile was willing to follow certain rules of purity.

Meanwhile, other Christians in the Jerusalem church did not think Peter and James had gone far enough. They insisted Gentiles must become circumcised and fully convert to Judaism in order to be saved (Acts 15:5). Paul thought of them as "false brothers" (Gal. 2:4), but in Acts, Luke did not. Luke seemed comfortable to call them "believers who belonged to the sect of the Pharisees" in the present tense (Acts 15:5 NRSV), just as Acts would later allow Paul to call himself a Pharisee in the present tense (Acts 23:6). When Paul returned to Jerusalem near the end of his ministry, less than ten years before the Jewish War began (A.D. 66), he came to a Jerusalem that was extremely zealous with nationalistic fervor, full of Christians of this stripe (Acts 21:20). The church of Jerusalem may very well have had members who participated militarily in that war for the full political independence of Israel.[10]

At the same time, the early church had individuals more liberal than Paul. At Corinth, he faced believers who were bold enough to eat at the temples of other gods (see 1 Cor. 8:10). These individuals looked to a preacher named Apollos as their hero (see 1 Cor. 1:12; 3:4; 4:6), which means Apollos may have had greater openness to such things than Paul.

The early church had its disagreements, and different groups within the church did things their way without interacting much with the other parts. The believers at Jerusalem were conservatives who had a hard time distinguishing their nationalistic fervor from their faith. Some American Christians might have this temptation today. Do we sometimes confuse patriotism and the American flag with the Christian gospel and flag (even though we have much less claim than the Jewish Christians of that day might have)? British and German believers would not consider their nations to have some sort of divine right, and no African or South American church would confuse itself with Israel in the Bible.

Paul was quite the liberal for his day, although there were ultra-liberals he sparred with also. Even though the Bible said that Israel was God's chosen people and laid down rules about purity and Israel's separation from the world, Paul dared to teach that the gospel was for everyone. He taught that non-Jews could be saved without fully converting to Judaism and thus fully following the only Scriptures they had. But we also find those who were even more radical than he was. Some at Corinth may have been proud they had a man who was sleeping with his step-mother (1 Cor. 5:1–2). How's that for not being under the Law, Paul? This church so incensed Paul that he wrote a letter so stern he at one point regretted even sending it (2 Cor. 7:8). Not surprisingly, no one preserved it, and it did not make it into the New Testament.

What we are seeing here is that the early church was much like the church today. There were conservative and liberal denominations. There were traditionalists who resisted change, and there were progressives who may have gone too far. There were disagreements over doctrine and practice. We know which groups God ended up rubber stamping, because their writings have ended up in the Bible. But it would not at all have been obvious to a neutral observer at the time. The Jerusalem Church would have been the best guess, with the dubious Paul as some radical out there on the fringes.

In our day-to-day lives, we have to make decisions on what to believe or do. We make those decisions as best we can. We talk to as many other believers as possible as we go along. We pray. We do our best as groups of believers to find our way through new territory. We have the benefit of two thousand years of hindsight, and we must have faith that God will eventually lead things to where they need to go. Our efforts will not undermine God's ultimate plan, and God does not need us to get the world where he wants it. He will use us or he won't. Part of faith is to realize that it does not all depend on us.

FOR FURTHER REFLECTION

1. Think back to when you first believed the Christian good news. Start a conversation with someone else and swap stories. Did either of your lives involve a major turn around? Should it have? If it did, have you retained that initial fervor when you changed? Why or why not? If you grew up in the church, is your fervor what you think it would have been if you had experienced a dramatic change? Why or why not?

2. Are you surprised to find so much conflict in the early church? To what extent do you agree with the reconstruction of Paul's missing years? To what extent do you think conflicts, even among Christians, are inevitable and not necessarily unhealthy? How do the disagreements among early Christians anticipate differences between denominations and churches today? Is such diversity always a bad thing? Why or why not?

3. To what extent would you say the leading of the Holy Spirit is better seen in hindsight than at the time you are making the key decisions? How do the controversies over Gentiles illuminate conflicts today over issues like women in the church and home?

4. To what extent would you say Christians might confuse patriotism with Christianity? For example, why do you think so many American churches have the American flag on their pulpits and treat Memorial Day as a Christian holiday? Could there ever be a human institution (a denomination or nation) that we could more or less equate with God's kingdom? What are the implications of distinguishing the secular from the sacred for how we might treat cultural elements of our lives (Mother's Day) differently from those that are historically Christian (Advent)?

4

LIFE BEYOND DEATH

THE HISTORICAL CONTEXT OF
PAUL'S FIRST LETTER TO THE THESSALONIANS

In the last chapter, we left Paul as he was preparing to depart on
another missionary journey around the year A.D. 49.[1] After they argued
over John Mark, Barnabas took his cousin and headed off for Cyprus
again, while Paul picked up a new partner named Silas and headed off
toward his home city of Tarsus in the region of Cilicia.

Paul and Barnabas may have agreed ahead of time to split the territory
they covered together in their earlier journey. Paul and Silas covered the
northern half, visiting cities like Derbe, Lystra, Iconium, and another
city named Antioch (of Pisidia), different from the Antioch of Syria
where they started. Most scholars think this is the region to which

Paul wrote the book of Galatians. Many conservative scholars think Paul wrote Galatians prior to this journey.

Paul's Later Journeys

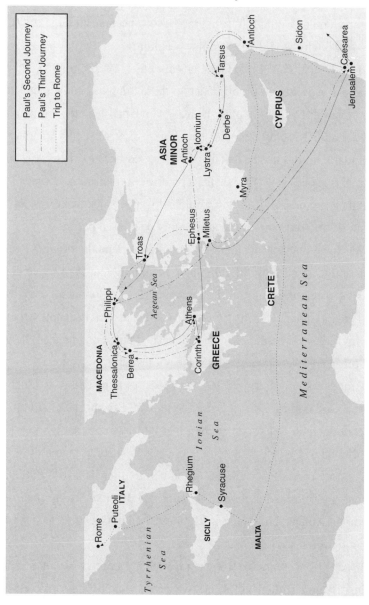

Paul's Second Journey
Paul's Third Journey
Trip to Rome

Antioch
Sidon
Tarsus
Caesarea
Jerusalem
CYPRUS
ASIA MINOR
Antioch
Iconium
Lystra
Derbe
Myra
Ephesus
Miletus
Troas
Aegean Sea
Philippi
Athens
CRETE
Mediterranean Sea
MACEDONIA
Thessalonica
Berea
Corinth
GREECE
Ionian Sea
Rhegium
Syracuse
SICILY
MALTA
Rome
Puteoli
ITALY
Tyrrhenian Sea

At Lystra, Paul and Silas met a young man named Timothy who accompanied them on the rest of the journey. Surprisingly, Acts also tells that Paul had him circumcised (16:3). Readers have no basis to doubt Acts about this claim, although it is curious. In Galatians, Paul argued Gentiles would fall from grace if they became circumcised (Gal. 5:2–4). So why would he circumcise Timothy?

If, as I think, Paul wrote Galatians after this time, he might still have been working through his approach to these things when he met Timothy. Nevertheless, Acts implies the reason Paul had Timothy circumcised was because Timothy's mother was Jewish (see Acts 16:1). It may be then that Paul did not have Titus circumcised because Titus was fully Gentile (see Gal. 2:3). This seems a plausible explanation. Perhaps Paul thought a circumcised Timothy would help him connect with Jews, while an uncircumcised Timothy would simply be unused potential.

Whatever practical advantages circumcising Timothy brought Paul, it apparently caused him difficulty later. Assuming that Paul wrote Galatians later than this point in time, some of Paul's opponents may have used Paul's circumcision of Timothy to claim that even Paul now believed circumcision was preferable (see Gal. 5:11). Paul reassured them he was still preaching that circumcision was unnecessary to salvation.

Paul eventually followed Roman roads north to Troas, and then he sensed God calling him to cross the narrow Bosphorus channel into Macedonia. Paul founded the church at Philippi, apparently one of his favorite churches. He founded the church at Thessalonica a little further west. According to Acts, he and Silas then headed south into Greece and founded a church in Berea (17:10–12). He stopped over shortly in Athens, but then quickly moved on to Corinth. He stayed in Corinth for almost two years.

In Acts 18, we learn the Roman governor at Corinth was a man named Gallio. By archaeological fortune, we can date Gallio's governorship in

Corinth to around A.D. 51–52. All in all, it fits very well with Acts to assume that Paul was in Corinth from around A.D. 50–52.

Paul's writings tell us little of his time in Philippi and Thessalonica and nothing of his time in Berea. Acts tells us he was jailed for a night in Philippi, that an earthquake hit the jail, and that he was freed the next day (16:25–40). First Clement, a letter written near the end of the first century by the leader of the Roman churches, mentions seven imprisonments of Paul (5.5). Though the letter does not carry the authority of Scripture, it may still give us accurate information about Paul. If Paul was imprisoned seven times, Philippi was probably his first or second imprisonment. If his earlier encounter with the Roman governor of Cyprus followed a similar night in jail (see Acts 13:7), his first imprisonment would have been in Cyprus. We cannot say with certainty.

Paul did not stay long at Thessalonica. Acts implies it might have been as few as three Saturdays (17:2), but it was probably at least a little longer. Philippians 4 indicates the church at Philippi sent him material support more than once while he was there. Also, while Acts focuses on the Jews and their opposition to Paul, 1 Thessalonians is overwhelmingly directed at Gentiles, implying that Paul's most fruitful ministry in the city was not in the synagogue. Perhaps Paul stayed there a couple of months, just long enough to get things started, although he leaves before he sees it come to fruition (see 1 Thess. 2:17).

For whatever reason, Paul did not stay long in Athens either. According to 1 Thessalonians 3:1–2, Paul and Silas sent Timothy back to Thessalonica from there.[2] They were worried about whether the church had been successfully launched. Paul wrote 1 Thessalonians after Timothy returned with news of the church. It is unknown whether Paul was already in Corinth at this point, but it seems reasonable, assuming Paul did not stay long in Athens.

Acts 17 records a brilliant speech by Paul to the Areopagus, the ruling council of the city. Paul may have spent another night or two in jail before seeing the council; if he did, it would be the second or third of his imprisonments. It seems Paul was charged with promoting an unfamiliar cult, a concern for the Roman leaders as great as homeland security might be for our leaders today. As in Thessalonica, the authorities in Athens seemed content for Paul to move on rather than face more severe punishment.

So, Paul penned 1 Thessalonians either at Athens or, perhaps more likely, at Corinth. I agree with the majority of scholars that 1 Thessalonians, in addition to being Paul's first surviving letter, is likely the first New Testament book that was written. One of the main topics of 1 Thessalonians is the fate of those who die before Christ returns. We will find that theme in some of Paul's other letters in subsequent chapters of this book.

OVERVIEW OF 1 THESSALONIANS

Ideas and logical statements are only a small part of our conversations with one another. Our communication functions as much on a relational and emotional level as on a logical one. Teachers of ancient rhetoric fully took these other dimensions of persuasion into account.[3] They called logical argument the *logos* mode of persuasion. Arguments that played on the emotions of the audience were built on *pathos*. A third mode of persuasion was built on *ethos*, persuasion based on trust toward the person doing the persuading.

The first three chapters of 1 Thessalonians are largely about establishing ethos between Paul and the Thessalonians. Paul built on the common experiences he and the Thessalonians shared, as well as the good will secured by Timothy's visit. He reassured them of his good motives and the broader struggle they had joined with God against evil.

The form of 1 Thessalonians is much like normal letters of the day.[4] The main differences are its length and how Paul expanded the typical greeting. Most letters began with a simple greeting, also called a pre-script: x to y, greetings. It is typical of Paul's letters to significantly expand the greeting to communicate more about himself and his readers. First Thessalonians, perhaps because it is Paul's earliest letter, expands the greeting the least of any of Paul's writings, adding a few words about the Thessalonian church and offering the characteristic Pauline blessing, "Grace and peace to you" (1:1) instead of the normal Greek salutation, which simply said, "Greetings." The word for grace (*charis*) is similar to the word for greetings (*chairein*), and Paul added the characteristic Jewish peace (*shalom*). Paul's "grace and peace" was thus a snapshot of his overall message which united Jew and Greek in Christ.

Letters usually had a thanksgiving or blessing section of some kind after the greeting. For example, the letter writer might invoke the favor of the gods on the audience. In 1:2–10, Paul thanked God for the Thessalonians and anticipated one of the key topics he would address later in the letter—Christ's return to earth (1:10). All of Paul's letters have something like this right after the greeting, except Galatians, where Paul perhaps intended to shame his readers by refraining from the usual thanksgiving. First Thessalonians also has some very brief closing remarks (5:12–24) and a postscript (5:25–28).

THE FATE OF CHRISTIANS WHO DIE

Although 1 Thessalonians addresses several issues, the central topic is the question of what happens to Christians who die before Christ returns (4:13—5:11). Before he addressed the big issue, Paul urged the Thessalonians to avoid sexual immorality (4:3–8). He also urged them to love one another with brotherly love (4:9–10) and to work diligently (4:11–12). Some scholars think the Thessalonians were so focused on Christ's return that they stopped going about the daily business of their lives. It is a fun suggestion, but we do not know for sure. Paul then dove into the main topic: Christ's coming return to earth.

It can be hard at first to understand the mindset of the Thessalonians. How could they not know what happens to Christians who died before Christ came back? Even though Paul was only in Thessalonica a brief time, you would still think they would have talked about eternal destiny. We are so familiar with some of these basic truths it is hard to put ourselves in the shoes of someone for whom these were radically new ideas. One popular soul-winning technique opens the conversation with the question, "Do you know for certain that if you died tonight you would go to heaven?"[5] The truth Paul addressed has become an obvious assumption for us.

RESURRECTION VERSUS IMMORTALITY

However, it may also be that some of our own assumptions are unexamined. For example, do we understand the difference between Paul's talk of resurrection and Plato's idea of the immortality of the soul? Resurrection in 1 Thessalonians was not something that happened at death, where humans continued to exist as spirit beings. Resurrection was viewed as an event that will take place when Jesus Christ returns to earth from heaven. The only one who has been resurrected up to this point in history was Jesus Christ himself. Even those Jesus raised to life were not resurrected in the same way Jesus was, because they eventually died again, to await the resurrection when Jesus returns.

RESURRECTION OF THE BODY

Resurrection for Paul also involved a body. This aspect of resurrection is particularly clear in 1 Corinthians 15, where Paul addresses similar issues with the Corinthians. "But someone will ask, 'How are the dead raised? With what kind of body do they come?'" (1 Cor. 15:35 NRSV). Embodiment is so central to the idea of resurrection for Paul that the possibility that some sort of body might not be involved did not even occur to him.

For Paul, this body was not like our current bodies: "flesh and blood cannot inherit the kingdom of God" (15:50 NRSV). Our body that dies is a natural or physical body (*psychikos*).[6] Our body that rises is, like Christ's, a spiritual body (*pneumatikos*). It is a body, so it is not just our spirit. It is a body with glory, perhaps not unlike the glory of heavenly bodies such as the stars, at least as they appear to us from the earth (15:40–41). Paul used the categories available to him to try to describe our heavenly bodies. These bodies, perhaps surprisingly to some of us, will be just like Christ's resurrection body. "Just as we have borne the image of the man of dust, we will also bear the image of the man of heaven" (1 Cor. 15:49 NRSV). In Philippians, Paul also said that Christ "will transform the body of our humiliation that it may be conformed to the body of his glory" (Phil. 3:21 NRSV).

RESURRECTION AND CHRIST'S RETURN

But how could these things not have come up while Paul was in Thessalonica? Did Paul just think the church needed reminding? His audience did seem to be overwhelmingly Gentile. It is hard to imagine that a group of Jews would have turned to God "from idols" (1 Thess. 1:9). Accordingly, they might not have known much of anything about the distinctively Jewish notion of resurrection. Most non-Jews at the time did not anticipate a meaningful afterlife.

But perhaps the best explanation is to recognize that Paul's preaching focused more on Christ's return to earth rather than on life after death. We tend to think we will die, even though Christ will return to earth one day. The order was probably reversed in Paul's earliest preaching. Christ is coming back to earth very soon, and—oh, yes—if you die before it happens, there is life after death.

We might picture a scenario where Paul preached that Jesus had died on the cross as an atoning sacrifice, an act of faithfulness that made it possible for anyone to be reconciled to the one true God, whether Jew or Gentile. God had also raised Jesus from the dead and enthroned him at his right hand, not only as the Jewish king, but as Lord over the whole world. Jesus would return from heaven very soon to take his rightful place as king over the world. The good news Paul preached was that the Thessalonians could escape the coming judgment if they were baptized in the name of Jesus. Baptism would appropriate the cross of Jesus and they would be saved from God's coming wrath (see 1 Thess. 1:9–10).

But then, perhaps, someone in Thessalonica died—someone who had believed in the gospel. The Thessalonians, dejected, thought "How sad! Uncle Demetrius was so excited to be part of the kingdom of God when Christ returned. But now he's dead and won't be able to see Jesus." So, Paul explained the nature of resurrection to them. "Don't worry. Uncle Demetrius is not lost. There will be a resurrection at the time of Jesus' return. The dead corpses will rise first, even before we who are alive and remain."

We see several interesting dynamics here. First, the word Paul used for dead had the sense of a dead body, a corpse. Paul was not talking about immortality of the soul, but rather corpses coming back to life. Second, he included himself and his audience when he spoke of "we who are alive and remain" (1 Thess. 4:17 NASB). In his letters, Paul never said outright, "I expect to be alive when Jesus returns," but his earliest letters especially give this impression, as do some other New Testament letters (see 1 Cor. 7:29; 1 Pet. 4:17). From this perspective, we can see that we must always live in expectation that Christ could come back soon. We are to live in imminent expectation of Christ's return.

Both Paul and the Thessalonians assumed some details that Paul did not mention explicitly. For example, Paul said that they "will be caught up in the clouds together with them to meet the Lord in the air" (1 Thess. 4:17 NRSV), the verse that stands behind the idea of a rapture. Paul concluded this verse with, "So we will be with the Lord forever" (NRSV). What Paul did not say, though, is where that forever will be. Many scholars believe we will meet Christ in the air like you go out to meet a king or important person coming to town. You then go back into town with them. Some passages, like 1 Corinthians 6:2, indicate Christians will participate in the judgment of the world. It therefore seems quite possible we will meet Christ only to come back to earth for the judgment.

A GENERAL RESURRECTION

Paul also only spoke of "the dead in Christ" being raised first (1 Thess. 4:16). Interestingly, the New Testament never says anywhere that all the dead will rise immediately at the point of Christ's initial return. Revelation puts the millennial reign of Christ between a first resurrection of Christian martyrs and a second, more general resurrection (Rev. 20:4–5). Meanwhile, Paul himself never clearly mentioned a second resurrection where all the rest of the dead, both righteous and wicked, would rise.

This is an interesting observation. As Christians, we believe in a general resurrection, when all the dead will rise, some to eternal life and some to an eternal judgment. But we have not taken this idea from Paul's writings. Paul never mentioned hell, although 2 Timothy 4:1 does mention that Christ will judge the dead, and Philippians 2:10 includes those "under the earth," the dead presumably, among all who will bow before Christ. But the idea of hell comes more from the books of Matthew and Revelation and Christian tradition.

Paul's writings hardly talk about the time when "every knee should bend, in heaven and on earth *and under the earth*, and every tongue should confess that Jesus Christ is Lord" (Phil. 2:10–11 NRSV, emphasis added). Certainly the living will bow before Christ when he returns to earth. But of the dead, Paul mostly focused on the dead in Christ who will rise. Perhaps Christian understanding in relation to a general resurrection was still in progress at this time. If, at this point, Paul only knew about the resurrection of those in Christ, it would explain the Thessalonians' disappointment.

It might also explain why some Christians were baptizing for the dead (1 Cor. 15:29). They were be trying to do the equivalent of what Judas Maccabeus did in a well known Jewish story of the time. In 2 Maccabees 12:43–45, Judas paid for sacrifices to be made for certain fallen soldiers so they could be part of the resurrection.[7] In the same way, some early Christians may have thought they could make sure their loved ones were included in the resurrection—maybe individuals who had never even heard of Jesus—by being baptized for them.

THE INTERMEDIATE STATE

Paul was also mostly silent on what happened to Christians in between their deaths and the resurrection. In 1 Thessalonians 4 and 1 Corinthians 15, Paul referred to the dead as those who have fallen "asleep" (see 1 Thess. 4:13; 1 Cor. 15:18). Accordingly, some have wondered if Paul had no sense of conscious afterlife in his earliest writings. Whether or not this is the case, by the time he wrote Philippians, Paul thought of death as departing to "be with Christ" (Phil. 1:23). Similarly, 2 Corinthians 5:6 said that being "at home in the body [is to be] away from the Lord." Whatever Paul started out thinking, his clearest statement in Philippians implied that the Christian is with Christ between death and the future resurrection, although Paul never said in what form.

Some scholars have also suggested that Paul's thought underwent development between 1 and 2 Corinthians on the question of when resurrection takes place.[8] In 1 Corinthians 15, Paul clearly thought of us receiving our resurrection body at the time of Christ's return. However, 2 Corinthians 5 says "that if the earthly tent we live in is destroyed" (5:1 NRSV), meaning if we die, then we have "a house not made with hands, eternal in the heavens" (5:1 NRSV), meaning our resurrection body. It would be easy to read this statement to indicate that we go to heaven when we die and get a spiritual body immediately at death. We want to please Christ whether here in the body or in heaven when we die (2 Cor. 5:9). And some scholars would argue that our appearance "before the judgment seat of Christ" in the next verse (5:10 NRSV) is what happens immediately at death.

Although this is a possible interpretation, most scholars have not opted for it. It is possible to interpret parts of Philippians and Romans with this slightly different understanding of the timing of resurrection (that is, that it takes place at death). But it does not seem the most natural reading of, for example, Philippians 3:11. These two letters were written about the same time or a little later than 2 Corinthians. Further, 2 Timothy 2:18 warns of those who say the resurrection has already happened. Could it be a warning against the kind of teaching we are talking about?

LIFE REFLECTIONS

Looking at these sorts of questions in detail can be a little startling. For example, popular thinking usually simplifies it to say that you die and then either go to heaven or to hell. Some equate the idea of the immortality of the soul with bedrock Christian faith so much that they might even react in anger to hearing what resurrection was really about in the Bible.[9] Meanwhile, the notion that we will reunite with our bodies is not attractive to many people today, just as it wasn't to some in Paul's time. The idea of resurrection was foolishness to some Greeks— they could not understand why they would want this "prison house of the soul" back.[10] The idea that the resurrection is an event still on the horizon can disrupt the comfortable sense some people have of dying and then immediately going to their final resting place.

Scholarly debates over the meaning of various passages can also be confusing, even disturbing. Even those who know the most about these issues find room in the evidence for disagreement. Did Paul's thought develop in some ways over time? It implies a rethinking of the assumption that the Bible is a single, static book that consistently says the same thing. It pushes us to read the Bible more as a library of books than a single one. We have to get a sense of the biblical trajectory rather than assume Genesis teaches exactly the same things as Revelation. For example, on this particular issue, the Old Testament has little to say about the afterlife at all (see Ps. 30:9; Eccl. 9:4–6). The only passage in the Old Testament that scholars agree points to a meaningful, personal, conscious life after death is Daniel 12:2–3. The New Testament thus seems to take us further along on a trajectory of revelation than the Old Testament on this issue.

Many of the beliefs we have on issues like the afterlife seem obvious to us in Scripture. But the reason is not always because it really is clear, but rather because of a certain common sense we have inherited from the Christian traditions of which we are a part. Some of these traditions are rather recent, like the idiosyncratic beliefs of churches that only came into existence in the last century or so. By contrast, the best common sense readings are those that the Christian Tradition (big T) arrived at by hashing out these sorts of ambiguities throughout the ages. Presumably, God's Holy Spirit has had something to do with such common Christian faith, such spiritual common sense.

On the afterlife, Christians have affirmed almost since the beginning, "I believe in . . . the resurrection of the body and the life everlasting."[11] We have affirmed this resurrection as something that is yet to come (except for Christ, the firstfruits of the dead; 1 Cor. 15:20) and will involve continuity with our human bodies as possible, although transformed into something that cannot decay. Christians throughout the centuries have affirmed that our souls will continue to exist and be conscious between our death and our resurrection.

Christian tradition throughout the centuries has generally looked to a similarly transformed creation, a new earth. Paul is not clear on where he thought we would spend eternity, but he did speak of the redemption of the creation along with the redemption of our bodies (Rom. 8:19–23). It is perhaps more likely than not that he saw us living out eternity on a new earth with new bodies (1 Cor. 15:50). Many Christians think of us spending eternity in heaven, and there are some New Testament passages that can be read this way (see John 14:3; Heb. 12:26–27; 1 Pet. 1:4; 2 Pet. 3:10). But throughout the centuries, more Christians have believed we would spend eternity on a new earth (see Rev. 21:2).

FOR FURTHER REFLECTION

1. To what extent would you say you read the Bible as logical revelation, as truths God is trying to impart to you? To what extent would you say you read the Bible to be changed by the encounter or to learn how to live? Ask God to help you see any imbalances in the way you read Scripture. What are some changes you might make in the way you read the Bible?

2. Evaluate your understanding of life after death in light of this chapter. Have you had a good understanding of what resurrection is, or has your view largely assumed only the immortality of the soul? How would you explain to a child what happens after we die?

3. To what extent would you say God continued to clarify Christian understanding on various topics even after the books of the New Testament were written (such as, hell, the judgment of all the dead, the Trinity)? Do you tend to think Christian tradition is a distraction and that things started to go downhill almost as soon as the Bible was written, or has God continued to meet Christians in their own times and places and to clarify Christian understanding?

DISUNITY AT CORINTH

GETTING TO CORINTH

Paul spent almost two years ministering at Corinth. His first converts were members of the household of Stephanus (1 Cor. 16:15), including Stephanus, Fortunatus, and Achaicus (16:17). Other converts included: Chloe (1:11), Crispus (1:14), Gaius (1:14), Erastus (Rom. 16:23), and Quartus (Rom. 16:23).[1] First Corinthians 1:1 mentioned a coauthor, Sosthenes, the name of the synagogue leader in Corinth who was beaten in Acts 18:17.

The conflict at Corinth between Jews who believed and those who did not played out in many parts of the Mediterranean world. Christianity was not yet a distinct religion but only one of many branches of Judaism at the time: Pharisees, Sadducees, Essenes, and Jesus-followers.[2] The first two groups were largely confined to Jerusalem; the Essenes may have spread out some. There is good reason to think that Jesus-followers regularly came into conflict with more mainstream Jews in the synagogues around the Mediterranean. For example, this kind of conflict in a Greek-speaking synagogue in Jerusalem seems to have resulted in Stephen getting stoned (Acts 6:9).

Two of Paul's most prominent coworkers, Priscilla and Aquila, were likely expelled from Rome along with all the Christian Jews of the city because of conflicts between Jesus-followers and mainstream Jews in the synagogues of the city.[3] Most scholars would date this conflict to around A.D. 49, which places Paul's work in Corinth around the years A.D. 50–52. As previously stated, this dating fits with the time when Gallio was proconsul in the city. Priscilla and Aquila had only recently entered the city when Paul first arrived there.

So, the synagogue at Corinth experienced similar conflict between Jews who believed Jesus was the Christ and those who did not. They had this conflict when Paul arrived in the city and a man named Crispus was synagogue leader (Acts 18:8). He believed in Jesus, and Paul mentioned him as someone he baptized there (1 Cor. 1:14), along with someone else named Gaius. Some scholars wonder if Gaius was the same person as the Titius Justus mentioned in Acts 18:7.[4] The synagogue at Corinth seemed to go through the same conflict again when a man named Sosthenes was synagogue leader (see Acts 18:17). This was likely the same person mentioned in 1 Corinthians 1:1. It was during this second conflict that Paul appeared before the Roman proconsul Gallio.

The place of judgment (or court) where Paul was accused by the Jews in Acts 18:12. In the background is the Acrocorinth, upon which a temple of Aphrodite once stood.

We hear of two further names in Romans 16:23, which Paul likely wrote from Corinth on a later visit. Erastus is called the city's administrator, possibly the city treasurer or perhaps director of public works. Among the ruins of Corinth, there is a sidewalk with an inscription that proclaims it was paid for by one Erastus, the city's "aedile," a position that generally fits how Paul described him.

Along with Gaius and Erastus, Romans 16:23 also sends the greetings of someone named Quartus. If we add the household of Chloe (1 Cor. 1:11), which may have included some of the people we have already mentioned, we have no less than nine names of local Corinthians who were associated with the church.

The Erastus Inscription. Erastus was the city administrator of Corinth named in Romans 16:23.

These nine names belong to at least three households and quite possibly more. We know of the household of Stephanus, of Chloe, and presumably of Gaius. Paul referred to the church at Corinth in the singular in the greeting of 1 Corinthians 1:1. From this fact, we should probably infer that the church at Corinth could meet in a single house, regardless of whether they sometimes broke into even smaller house churches. Since in Romans 16:23, Paul said the whole church enjoyed the hospitality of Gaius, it seems quite possible that he was somewhat wealthy and could welcome the entire church of forty to fifty people in his house for worship.

In 1 Corinthians 1:26, Paul says "not many" of the Corinthians were influential or of noble birth. But individuals like Gaius and Erastus were likely among the few who were. Erastus must have been a Roman citizen of some means to serve in public office and fund service projects. If Gaius was Titius Justus, he would presumably have been a Roman citizen as well. This sort of social status created in itself temptations and pressures that most of the believers, who did not have such status, would not have had to face.

At some point after Paul's run-in with the Roman proconsul Gallio, Paul departed from Corinth. Acts tells us he briefly visited Ephesus before sailing to Jerusalem, traveling back to Antioch in the north of Palestine, and then revisited the churches he had founded throughout Asia Minor (Acts 18:23). Paul left little trace of this trip in any of his letters.[5] But eventually, perhaps in A.D. 53 or 54, he found himself back in Ephesus, which he set up as his base camp for ministry over the next three years or so.

Paul's Later Journeys

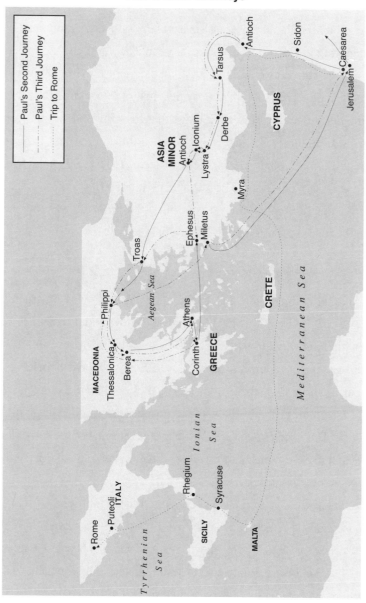

ISSUES AT EPHESUS AND CORINTH

By the time Paul arrived at Ephesus, Priscilla and Aquila had been ministering at Corinth for perhaps a year. They already had one very significant convert to faith in Christ, an eloquent Jew from Alexandria named Apollos. This incident provides insight into some of the details of the early church. Acts 18:18 says that Priscilla and Aquila (rather than Aquila and Priscilla) invited him to their home and explained Christ to him. In other words, the wife seems to have taken the lead in the conversion of Apollos. Priscilla is mentioned first in both Acts and Paul's letter, and most often it is implied that Priscilla was the one to take the lead (see Acts 18:26; Rom. 16:3).[6]

FOLLOWERS OF JOHN THE BAPTIST

Another item of interest is that Acts says Apollos was "instructed in the way of the Lord" (18:25) but did not know about Jesus. He only knew of John the Baptist. What makes this comment very interesting is the Essenes at Qumran on the Dead Sea also saw themselves as preparing the way of the Lord. The Essenes applied the same passage from Isaiah 40 to themselves as the gospels use to describe John the Baptist.[7] There are enough similarities between some of the early Christians and these Essenes that I wonder if there was some overlap at first between the two groups.[8]

Acts tells us that Paul also encountered these followers of John the Baptist when he came to Ephesus (Acts 19:1–7). The book of Acts makes it very clear that John's baptism was not yet Christian baptism. Paul baptized these followers in the name of Jesus and laid hands on them so they would receive the Holy Spirit—something John's baptism did not provide. Here, we find hints of an important need in the early church to distinguish Jesus' followers from mere followers of John the Baptist.

John baptized with water, but Jesus baptized with the Holy Spirit (see Mark 1:8). The Holy Spirit thus indicates that a person is truly going to be saved from the coming judgment. If we add hints from the gospel of John, it looks like the followers of Jesus and the followers of John the Baptist came into some conflict at Ephesus. According to tradition, the gospel of John originated at Ephesus. Its portrayal of John the Baptist is fascinating in that it consistently downplays his significance. For example, the gospel of John never actually mentions that Jesus submitted to baptism by John. Unlike Matthew 11:14, John the Baptist himself denies that he is Elijah in John 1:21. Only in the book of John do we hear of John the Baptist's followers leaving him to follow Jesus while John is still alive and baptizing (John 1:37). All these hints probably add up to a group of followers of John the Baptist's teaching at Ephesus who had not come to believe that Jesus was the Messiah.

TOLERANCE OF SEXUAL IMMORALITY

It was not long after Paul left Corinth that the church there began to have issues. Perhaps those issues had been in play even before Paul left the city.[9] The first we hear about is a problem with those in the Corinthian church who were sexually immoral. Although we call 1 Corinthians "First" Corinthians, it was not actually the first letter Paul sent this church from Ephesus.[10] In 1 Corinthians 5:9, Paul mentions a letter he had previously sent them even before 1 Corinthians. In that letter, he had told them "not to associate with sexually immoral people" (5:9).

Perhaps he had been somewhat general or vague in that letter, hoping they would get the hint.[11] Alas, they did not. He had to spell it out—he had in mind people who were actually part of their fellowship who were sexually immoral. He continued to mention a host of people who should not be part of the church's fellowship—people whose lives might be aptly described as full of greed, slander, drunkenness, or dishonesty; there were those who participated in pagan worship or whose pattern of life was full of sexual immorality (5:11). In keeping with what it meant to eat together with others at that time, Paul told the Corinthian believers not to eat with such individuals as part of their fellowship (5:11).

LACK OF UNITY

However, the key issue that led Paul to write 1 Corinthians—the second letter Paul wrote this church—was disunity. We might aptly consider 1 Corinthians 1:10 the key verse of the entire letter: "Now I appeal to you, brothers and sisters, by the name of our Lord Jesus Christ, that all of you be in agreement and that there be no divisions among you, but that you be united in the same mind and the same purpose" (NRSV). In most of the varied issues Paul discussed in the rest of 1 Corinthians, one can hear the not-so-subtle subtext of division in the congregation.

Because of the group orientation of most people at the time, we would expect that many of these divisions at Corinth involved the same people, despite the fact that the issues vary. Independent thinking was not valued much in the ancient world but rather loyalty to your people and to your group. We would therefore be surprised if most of these divisions on issues at Corinth did not largely involve the same people.

These divisions probably had a great deal to do with the social status—or at least the social aspirations—of the people involved. This dynamic comes out particularly with the issue of food sacrificed at pagan temples. The poor did not generally have access to meat except on the occasion of city festivals. And it was common practice to segregate dining fellowship by social class—sometimes even involving a different menu depending on status.[12] Further, the poor probably could resist the temptation to eat at a pagan temple more easily than individuals like Erastus, who apparently tried to climb the city's social ladder. He probably experienced pressure to see and be seen at important civic events relating to the city's temples.

But whatever the underlying dynamics of these divisions were, they looked on the surface like allegiances to different Christian leaders. Paul wrote, "It has been reported to me by Chloe's people that there are quarrels among you, my brothers and sisters. What I mean is that each of you says, 'I belong to Paul,' or 'I belong to Apollos,' or 'I belong to Cephas,' or 'I belong to Christ'" (1:11–12 NRSV). As is so often the case, the presenting issue merely scratched the surface of the deeper interpersonal conflicts.

Those who were loyal to Paul were probably mostly the foundational stratum of the church, those who believed in Jesus while Paul ministered there. But Apollos followed Paul and, like so often today, the second pastor may not have looked at every issue quite the same way as the first. For example, Apollos was from Alexandria in Egypt and seems to have been a little more educated than Paul—at least in terms of Greco-Roman education. It is possible some of the divisions at Corinth represented differences between his and Paul's perspectives. After all, the two did not meet each other until after Apollos had ministered in Corinth.

Perhaps Apollos had been able to reach people from a higher socioeconomic status than Paul. One night hear Apollos' voice in the notion that "no idol in the world really exists" (1 Cor. 8:4 NRSV). If such were the case, it might help explain why Paul affirmed this idea in 1 Corinthians 8, while also claiming that demons inhabit pagan temples in 1 Corinthians 10:20. The first was Apollos' voice; the second Paul's. Paul did not want to contradict Apollos' teaching but qualify it so the Corinthians would take the appropriate course of action.

It could be that the Apollos group thought they knew more than the Paul group. Perhaps the Apollos group was saying, "All of us possess knowledge" (8:1 NRSV). Are the upper crust, the social ladder climbers of the Corinthian church, allowed to get away with sexual practices that were rejected even by Greek society? Is it wives from among the elite who, in 1 Corinthians 7 and 11, are using Christianity as an opportunity to free themselves of their husbands? Are these the people who are getting drunk during the Lord's Supper while others go away hungry? And, although it contradicts our modern biases, are these the individuals who think of themselves as "spiritual" (see 3:1), who are speaking in tongues and looking down on others in the church who do not (14:1)?

Those who had knowledge (8:1) and thought of themselves as spiritual (3:1) and wise (1:20, 30; 2:1, 6) were likely also those who took others in the church before Roman courts (6:1–11). In one of the most sarcastic comments in the letter, Paul asked the Corinthians if there was no one "wise enough" in the church to resolve the dispute over which they took each other to court (6:5). Instead, they exposed the good name of Christ to public disgrace and gave worldly powers authority in God's church. Once again, the aggressive party seemed to line up with the primary troublemakers in the community across the board.

The primary tension in the congregation seems to have been between those who were loyal to Paul and those who were using Apollos as an excuse to behave in a different way than Paul instructed. Though Peter and Christ were mentioned in the opening line of this letter (1:12), it was Paul and Apollos whose names popped up most in the early part of the letter (see 3:4–6; 4:6). A division between those who were loyal to Paul and those who championed Apollos may have thus stood at the heart of the divisions at Corinth, which will be explored in more detail in chapter 7 of this book.

It seems less likely there was a distinctive "Peter group" or a "Christ group" following the divisions Paul mentioned in 1:12. However, some Jewish believers at Corinth may not have ranked Paul as highly as Peter (see 9:5), and Paul did mention Peter again as a possible source of division in 3:22.[13] Remember from Galatians 2 that Paul and Peter did not see eye-to-eye on every issue. In particular, if the letter in Acts (specifically verses 15:23–29) already existed by the time Paul wrote 1 Corinthians, it is suspiciously conspicuous that Paul never mentioned its contents to the Corinthians.

The statement "I belong to Christ" (1 Cor. 1:12 NRSV) may be a slam at the Jerusalem apostles themselves, who knew Jesus while he was on earth and were the first whom Christ commissioned. Paul was, in effect, saying that individuals like Peter and James were no more authoritative than Paul was. Certainly, this is the position he took in Galatians 2, where he referred to Peter, James, and John as so-called pillars (2:6) and claimed it didn't really matter to him what they were because God did not show favoritism (nor does he show it today).

The first six chapters of 1 Corinthians thus seem to deal directly with rumors Paul heard from members of Chloe's household (1:11; see also 11:18). Perhaps while Paul was in the middle of drafting the letter, Stephanus and others also arrived with a letter from the Corinthians. Paul thus dedicated the second half of the letter (1 Cor. 7–16) to answering questions the Corinthians sent him. Chapter 7 addresses questions about sex within marriage and whether virgins should marry. Chapters 8–10 answers questions on meat sacrificed at pagan temples. Chapters 12–14 deal with spiritual gifts, and chapter 16 with the collection for Jerusalem, as well as with the question of Apollos.

LIFE REFLECTIONS

First Corinthians is one of those books where the instructions often jump right off the page of the Bible and into our lives. Not all of the biblical books are this way. They were, after all, not originally written directly to us but to a myriad of different ancient contexts. True, it was the same God speaking to them as to us, and so, as Christians, we believe all these books are for us even though they were not originally to us. God can meet us in these words even when we have little sense of their original meaning.

The fundamental problem of the Corinthian church was disunity, driven by fundamental human desires like sex, power, and pride. I will address the various challenges at Corinth relating to sex in the next chapter of this book. Then in chapter 7, I will mention some of the specific issues on which they were divided, like what they should eat and how they should worship. An underlying factionalism lay behind these debates, an underlying dynamic of one group thinking it was better than another. Along with this party spirit, this "us versus them" mentality, there was a thirst for control and power. It is into this mix that Paul asserted his authority as an apostle.

POWER STRUGGLES

One of the reasons 1 Corinthians seems so directly relevant to the church today is the fact that division and factional pride remain perennial problems in congregations across the world. One of the key features of American Christianity is the church split, where one part of a congregation gets disgruntled with another part and leaves with a bunch of people because they do not have enough power to get their way. Even in congregations that stay together, someone probably will immediately spring to mind at the words *church boss*. Who is the person or family you need to get on your side if you want to do anything in your church—even if you are the pastor? Humans tend to be herd animals and prone to tribalism of a negative sort. The church is not immune.

The lessons of 1 Corinthians are still relevant to today's church power struggles. Some believers may have more authority than others in the church, but no one has greater status than any other. All the parts of the body of Christ should be equally valued, even if we all have different roles to play. At God's table, it does not matter whether you are the employee or employer (slave or free), whether you are male or female, whether you are the tribe in power or the one with less earthly status (Jew or Gentile).[14] God wants to give everyone the same menu at his table.

Everyone is expendable. A church whose health is tied to a single individual is not a healthy church nor can that person be a good leader. Churches often fall into hero worship. One sign of an unhealthy church is when its attendance drops off dramatically after a particular pastor or leader leaves. Such leaders sometimes mistake their following for importance or God's favoritism. Their gifts are God's grace toward them, but God does not play favorites. In God's eyes, their gifts do not increase their status, since they did nothing to get those God-given gifts in the first place. The humble soul who is truly thankful for the one thing God has enabled him or her to do is more worthy than a thousand powerful leaders of great influence who think they are special in God's eyes for abilities they did nothing to earn.

The conflict between followers of a previous pastor and a new one will be familiar to many churchgoers. In the case of the Corinthians, Apollos had left, and Paul was an apostle. At the time, however, Paul's apostleship and authority were not nearly as obvious as it is to us looking back. Paul needed the Spirit to convince his churches of his authority just as we need the Spirit today. Viewed from our human perspective, Paul had to demonstrate the validity of his call and spiritual authority just as we have to do today.

SPIRITUAL PRIDE

Some of the Corinthians thought they were more spiritual than others, even though they were far from it. Today, we would rarely say such a thing to others in the church. We know we are not supposed to say we are more spiritual than others.[15] But there are plenty in the church who think they are better than others when they are plainly not.

I come from a Christian tradition that has emphasized the importance of Christlike living and real-life transformation. But my tradition went through a period where external appearance was sometimes confused with real heart change. Whether a person dressed a certain way or wore a wedding ring was mistaken for love, joy, peace, and the true fruits of the Spirit. How ironic to hear someone looking down at someone else as being unspiritual because they were wearing jewelry. The very spirit betrayed a much more sinister unspirituality in that person's heart.

Again, there are different roles to be played in the church and in the world, but for Christians, they should not be connected to whether we are a "Jew or Greek . . . slave or free . . . male [or] female" (Gal. 3:28 NRSV). Most Christians today are comfortable with the first two comments, although some think we should distinguish differing roles in the church and the home based on gender. We will discuss God's ideal on this issue when we get to chapter 7.[16]

SPIRITUAL PREJUDICE

When we apply the distinctions between slave and free and Jew and Greek today, we find principles most of us might agree with until we get down to specifics. We might agree that it should make no difference whether a Christian is British or American. But, do we get a little more uncomfortable, maybe even irritated, when we ask if a Mexican, Palestinian, or Haitian Christian is just as precious in God's sight as the nice, middle-class, U.S.-born citizens on our church boards? And Christians regularly indulge in plenty of denominational condescension.

The New Testament does imply there are levels of reward in the kingdom (see 1 Cor. 3:10–15; 2 Cor. 5:10; Rom. 2:6–10). But these rewards are not based on our abilities or talents, nor are they based on our innate goodness. They are based on the degree to which we submit ourselves to God's power, enabling us to become Christlike in our thoughts and lives. Needless to say, thinking ourselves more spiritual or more important to God than others is hardly something God will reward.

Division is thus one of the fundamental problems that 1 Corinthians as well as the whole New Testament addresses. And it remains just as much a problem today as it was two thousand years ago. Division is trickier than adultery or murder, not least because we often have a way of telling ourselves we are divided over principles. "I am against you because you are wrong on how to live," or "I am against you because your understanding is wrong." We may be right, but probably just as often, we are wrong.

No matter what, it seems clear that we must love not only our enemies, but our Christian brothers and sisters as well. Perhaps on a rare occasion, groups within a congregation might agree to disagree and part company, but the vast majority of church splits have not fallen into this category. And those who are thinking of leaving their mainstream denomination should be mindful of what their absence will facilitate among those who remain, even if their leadership does seem to have strayed.

FOR FURTHER REFLECTION

1. Are there factions in your church? Being very tactful and maintaining a loving spirit, ask yourself where there might be a divisive spirit in your church? Ask yourself if you are part of any such divisions. If you are, what are you going to do to unify the spirit of your congregation?

2. Do you think it is ever appropriate for a church to split? If so, what is the proper point and why? How many of the thousands and thousands of church splits would you guess were actually legitimate, and how many were simply people being selfish or hateful?

3. Does your church inappropriately value status, wealth, or any earthly characteristic over what God actually values—love of God and love of neighbor? Without adding to the problem, what are some concrete steps you could take to move in the right direction, starting with yourself?

4. Do you think it is possible to use what you believe is true or how you think Christians should behave as an excuse for an ungodly and divisive attitude toward others? Examine your own attitudes to see if you have fallen into using truth and holiness as an ungodly weapon that undermines the body of Christ.

6

HOW NOT
TO HAVE SEX

While the first six chapters of 1 Corinthians address rumors Paul had heard about divisions at Corinth, the second half answers questions the Corinthians had sent to him in a letter, probably delivered by a man named Stephanus (see 1 Cor. 16:17). Here, I will focus on the first set of questions, which had to do with sex and marriage. Paul signaled the first in 7:1, "Now concerning the matters about which you wrote: 'It is well for a man not to touch a woman'" (NRSV).[1] Throughout the rest of the letter, we can tell when Paul was responding to a question by the phrase, "Now concerning" (1 Cor. 7:1, 25; 8:1; 12:1; 16:1, 12 NRSV).

MARITAL RELATIONS

Paul's first response may seem odd—"it is well for a man not to touch a woman" (NRSV). Did Paul really believe this statement? Most scholars think this was a quote from the letter sent by the Corinthians that Paul was acknowledging in his response. In other words, someone at Corinth was arguing that the ideal was for men not to have sex with women. What is striking is that Paul agreed; he conceded their point.

Paul's overall tactic in 1 Corinthians was to start where his audience was and then to move them in the right direction. So, the fact that Paul affirmed this statement may not fully indicate what he really thought. He was perhaps using tact, agreeing with them as much as he could to earn a hearing, so he could begin to modify their thinking.

If that was Paul's response, what was the original question? It was not about whether two people should get married, as the NIV assumes in its translation of 7:1. Instead, the question was whether married couples themselves should continue to have sex. Verse 3 makes this fact clear: "The husband should give to his wife her conjugal rights, and likewise the wife to her husband" (NRSV). When the Corinthians asked about touching a woman, they were discussing whether a man should have sex with his wife. Paul responded that, because of temptation, "each man should have his own wife"—have sex with her—"and each woman have her own husband"—have sex with him (7:2 NRSV).

That Christian husbands and wives would even question if a husband should "touch a woman" (7:1 NRSV) is completely foreign to us today and a clear indication that Paul was writing to an audience in a very different time and place. Paul considered celibacy the best option, probably because, at this time, he still thought Christ would return within their lifetime (1 Cor. 7:7). The impact of his thinking continues in the Roman Catholic Church today where priests are not allowed to marry. For the early Paul, widows ideally would not remarry (1 Cor. 7:39–40); and divorced men ideally would not remarry (7:27), although Paul told them they would not sin if they did. Virgins also would not sin if they got married (7:28).

Paul's treatment of sex here is thus very practical. He did not give the lofty thoughts on marriage in 1 Corinthians that we later find in Ephesians 5:22–33. Marriage in 1 Corinthians is a way of channeling sexual desire so that we do not seek sex elsewhere. People should get married so that they do not look for sex with prostitutes (1 Cor. 6:15–18) or burn with passion (7:9) toward virgins, thus wronging the virgin and her family (see 1 Thess. 4:5–6). Within marriage, husband and wife should have regular sex with each other so that neither is tempted to commit adultery (7:1–7).

Paul's instructions in this chapter are curious. What exactly was going on at Corinth? What line of reasoning would bring these sorts of questions? Curiosity grows as one continues to read the chapter. For example, Paul's instructions on divorce focused on the wife rather than the husband (1 Cor. 7:10–11). This is a little strange, especially since Paul said his teaching came directly from Jesus (7:10; see also Mark 10:11–12). It is not entirely clear that a woman was even able to divorce her husband in Palestine at the time of Christ. Assuming Jesus told wives not to leave their husbands, his teaching would have almost certainly focused on a husband not divorcing his wife.[2] Why the strange emphasis on wives initiating the divorce when Jesus' focus would have been on the husbands?

Further, most discussions end with comments that wrap up or summarize the main takeaway from the discussion. So, it is curious that 1 Corinthians 7 ends with the importance of women staying with their husbands until death: "A wife is bound as long as her husband lives. But if the husband dies, she is free to marry anyone she wishes, only in the Lord. But in my judgment she is more blessed if she remains as she is" (7:39–40 NRSV). What was going on at Corinth that led to these questions and, even more, these answers?

The answers to this question cannot be settled with any certainty. At the very least, the Corinthians did not associate sex with God's coming kingdom, and it is possible they got the idea from Paul. Jesus implied similar things: "when they rise from the dead, they neither marry nor are given in marriage, but are like angels in heaven" (Mark 12:25 NRSV). Perhaps some of them saw this teaching as an encouragement or excuse to stop having sex right away. Paul did not correct the idea; he just did not think it would work in practice.

Perhaps, given Paul's instruction that women not leave their husbands, some of the Corinthian women were using the gospel as an excuse to leave their husbands or at least not to have sex. Are these the same women who wanted to remove their veils (1 Cor. 11)—in a sense, wanted to take off their wedding rings? If 1 Corinthians 14:34–35 was in the original version of this letter, it might refer to the same group of disruptive individuals.

First Corinthians 7:25 addressed a related question: If celibacy was the ideal and Christ would return very soon, should virgins even consider marrying? In keeping with the culture of his day, Paul left the decision up to the man. Though the Greek text of 7:36–38 is somewhat ambiguous, most translations interpret it as a man making the decision whether to marry or not, so that Paul said the man wouldn't sin if he married his fiancé, but he would do even better not to marry her. The New American Standard Bible (NASB) offers a different perspective, in which a father is deliberating whether to give his virgin daughter away in marriage. The Greek grammar slightly favors the NASB translation, but most interpreters now favor the NIV translation.

Although some disagree, most scholars recognize the strong expectation in 1 Corinthians 7 that Jesus would return to earth very soon.

Most think that the "impending crisis" (7:26 NRSV) refers to the troubles about to take place around the time of Christ's return. First Peter has a similar expectation: "The time has come for judgment to begin with the household of God; if it begins with us, what will be the end for those who do not obey the gospel of God?" (1 Pet. 4:17 NRSV). The further we go into Paul's writings, the less we sense the immediacy of Christ's return. Most Christian traditions do not put a primacy on celibacy as Paul does in this chapter. First Timothy actually speaks against those who would forbid marriage (1 Tim. 4:3) and reverses Paul's ideal in 1 Corinthians 7:39–40 that widows remain unmarried (1 Tim. 5:9–16).

DIVORCE AND REMARRIAGE

In the midst of answering questions about sex and marriage, Paul addressed an underlying issue: divorce and remarriage. Paul's statements in 1 Corinthians 7 addressed a concrete, real-life situation. Paul was not simply giving timeless, universal statements, even if they come close. Remember that Paul made these statements in the middle of an argument, and arguments make us emphasize things we would not necessarily emphasize in a different context.

The Corinthian context thus helps us to understand why Paul seemed to give unequal instructions to men and women in 1 Corinthians 7. Paul prohibited divorce for both husbands and wives (7:10–11). But his instructions on remarriage seemed different depending on whether the husband or the wife is addressed. Paul did not advise divorced women to remarry (7:10–11). But then later in the same chapter, he advised a divorced husband to remarry, even though it was not the ideal (7:28).[3]

Christians have tended to miss the spirit of Jesus' teaching on divorce and remarriage, ironically making from Jesus' words a legalism that is diametrically opposed to the spirit of Jesus in relation to the Law elsewhere. We are eager to hear Jesus doing away with the Jewish food laws (see Mark 7:19). We "Amen" when he gets on the Pharisees for complaining that Jesus' followers are ignoring the Sabbath rules (see Mark 2:23–27). We are more than happy to dismiss the Levite and the priest for avoiding a bloody and dying Samaritan (see Luke 10:29–37), probably for reasons of Levitical purity. But we sometimes flip on the matter of divorce and make it an unpardonable sin, taking the role of the Pharisees in these gospel stories. There are some Christian denominations where a person can never officially become a member of a church if he or she has been divorced or remarried after a divorce. This is quite puzzling, though Jesus' teaching on divorce does seem, at least at first glance, more rigid than his other teachings, just as Paul's teaching on sex is more rigid than other particulars of the Old Testament Law.

We should picture in these instructions the same spirit of compassion that Jesus showed throughout the gospels. Are we really to think the Jesus who so emphasized, "The sabbath was made for humankind, and not humankind for the sabbath" (Mark 2:27 NRSV) suddenly switched to "humanity was made for the divorce rule, not the divorce rule for humanity"? Surely, Jesus' instructions to men not to leave their wives were targeted in compassion for the powerless women who would thereby be set adrift without anchor in a man's world. Is it any coincidence that Jesus' teaching on divorce in Matthew 5 seems a corollary to his teaching on adultery, as if divorce was simply a legal way of committing adultery?

As previously mentioned, Paul seemed to have two different sets of instructions for men and women in 1 Corinthians 7. In the beginning of the chapter, he told separated women to be reconciled to their husbands or else remain single (7:11). Later in the chapter, he advised a divorced man not to remarry but told him that he did not sin if he did remarry

(7:27–28). The NIV translation here is quite misleading. Paul did not say, "Are you unmarried?" in 7:27, as if the situation was whether virgins should marry at all. A better translation would be, "Have you been loosed from a wife? Do not seek a wife. But even if you should marry, you have not sinned." In other words, Paul allowed a man to remarry, even though it was not optimal, and advised against a woman remarrying.

The reason the NIV did not translate the verse this way is that Christians over time have, perhaps without realizing it, steadily applied Christian principles equally to both men and women. The fact that Paul did not is a good indication of the cultural dimension of his teaching here. The consequences of a woman divorcing and remarrying in the first century were more severe than the consequences of a man doing the same. In that sense, in some areas, we are able to live out the principles of the gospel more fully than the early church was. This is a difficult concept to grasp, since so many today have an idealistic and unrealistic picture of what the early church was actually like.

VISITING PROSTITUTES

For Paul, it was not the act of sex itself but the potential defilement that came from particular sex connections that made sex such a matter of concern. Paul did not tell a Corinthian man who might visit a prostitute that he must marry the prostitute. Paul did not tell him to remain single until all the other partners of the prostitute have died so that he could marry her. This entire line of thinking, which naturally flows from a sex-equals-marriage view, was completely foreign to Paul. The problem, in Paul's mind, was that visiting a prostitute made a bad connection, one that defiled and spoiled the church. It connected a circuit that shouldn't have been and short-circuited the system.

Paul did not have a dreamy or idealistic view of sex. He viewed it as a potential liability to be controlled. He may not have even known exactly how a man who slept with his step-mother defiled the church (1 Cor. 5). He just knew it defiled the church. He said Christians should not even eat with such persons because it would bring sickness and infection into the body of Christ. Similarly, Paul might not have been able to say why men having sex with men defiled the body of Christ, but it seems he firmly maintained that all the sexual acts of Leviticus 18 caused defilement.

It can be difficult for us to grasp the first-century mindset about adultery. People in the Mediterranean world did not consider a man's adultery as an offense against his own wife. Sleeping with a prostitute was not considered adultery. Adultery was the offense caused to another man by sleeping with the man's wife. Refraining from adultery had to do with men honoring other men; it was a kind of social contract by which men rested their minds from the fear that some other man might sleep with his wife behind his back. It also helped maintain social stability, keeping men from fighting or warring against other families to regain their honor. And it avoided questions of legitimacy in who might inherit property.

You can see, then, how differently Paul's instructions might have been received in his own day compared to ours. This is not always a bad thing. It may sometimes show that the revolutionary trajectory of the kingdom has shaped the church and society more than perhaps even Paul imagined. It may actually mean that God has, even without us knowing it, moved us closer to the fundamental social structure of the kingdom, where women count exactly as much as men do. We now recognize that a man commits adultery against his wife, not just a woman against her husband or a man against another man.

This distinction between the way we read the text and the way people did in the first century is a new thought for some of us, especially if we think we have simply been reading the Bible and doing what it says. But we should recognize that the Spirit has often led us to subtly contemporize Paul's words, usually with the help of solid Christian tradition.

HOMOSEXUAL SEX

Paul's writings engage the question of homosexual sex three times, and they are the only certain mentions of the topic in the New Testament (Rom. 1:24–27; 1 Cor. 6:9; 1 Tim. 1:10).[4] Clearly, the significance of this issue for us today is disproportionate to its biblical coverage, perhaps in part because it was not a matter of great controversy either in ancient Israel or the early Church. Nevertheless, those few places in the Bible that engage the subject all take the same position. In 1 Corinthians 6:9 in particular, Paul included those who practiced homosexual sex in a list of individuals who will not inherit the kingdom of God.

First Corinthians 6:9 and 1 Timothy 1:10 both use a word that does not appear anywhere else prior to Paul's writings, the Greek *arsenokoites*, meaning "male-bedders." Although it is hard to know for sure, Jews probably coined this word on the basis of the two key places in the Old Testament where homosexual sex is mentioned: Leviticus 18:22 and 20:13. Those passages prohibit a male lying with a male as a male lies with a female. An *arsenokoites* is thus someone whose lifestyle is typified by this practice.

Note the focus on the practice of homosexual sex. The places where the Bible mentions homosexual sex all have to do with the act of sex rather than with people who have a particular sexual orientation. Leviticus 18:22 and 20:13 are clearly directed at the practice of homosexual sex. The story of Sodom and Gomorrah (Gen. 19:4–11) as well as the Levite in Benjamin (Judg. 19:22–26) have to do with an act of homosexual rape that the men of each particular city wished to commit. In the second instance, the men go on to rape the man's concubine to death.

It is faulty interpretation to simply equate the people in these stories with individuals attracted to the same sex today. Homosexual rape and pederasty are quite different acts from most homosexual practices today and should be strongly distinguished. Further, although the Bible clearly rejects homosexual sex, its mention of Sodom and Gomorrah focused as much or more on the disgraceful way the city of Sodom and the city in Benjamin received strangers into their midst (Matt. 10:11–15). Here is another instance where, without knowing it, we may tend to read a biblical story with different glasses than the ancient audiences did.

The mention of homosexual sex in the New Testament similarly focuses on the act rather than on orientation. This is certainly the case in Romans 1, where Paul wrote of men with men and women with women, focusing on the act of sex. The word *arsenokoites* is used for those whose lives were typified by homosexual sex. The other word Paul used in 1 Corinthians 6:9 also likely focuses on a sex act, the Greek *malakos*. This word means "soft" and so would be the best candidate for a word that referred to someone who was "effeminate" in general, as the KJV translated the word.

But the NIV probably comes closer when it translates the word as "male prostitute," relating it to a person who plays a passive role in homosexual sex. In the end, the notion of a person having a particular orientation, being intrinsically attracted to one or the other sex, is a fairly modern conception. Prior to the 1800s, people attracted to the same sex would still likely be married to the opposite sex and have children. Homosexual sex was thus seen as an activity engaged in on the side, beyond marriage to the opposite sex, rather than as another kind of sexuality. The very notion of us having a particular kind of sexuality is a fairly recent way of thinking.

Paul's main problem with homosexual sex was probably like the problem he had with visiting a prostitute or sleeping with your stepmother (1 Cor. 5)—it infected or defiled the body of Christ. In Romans 1, Paul used homosexual sex as an example of God letting the world go, abandoning it to spiral out of control after it failed to glorify him as God and instead turned to worshiping idols resembling the creation (Rom. 1:24, 26). Paul said that such individuals "received in their own persons the due penalty for their error" (Rom. 1:27 NRSV). This statement should not be connected to AIDS or venereal diseases—Paul and his audiences would not be thinking this sort of thing. Paul told us the penalty he had in mind in the same sentence when he called the practice "shameless acts" (NRSV). He was likely saying that the shame of the act itself carried its own due penalty.

We should be careful when applying the Bible's teaching on homosexual sex. We have so much emotion tied up in this issue that it is all too easy to use the Bible as an excuse for un-Christlike attitudes. The fundamental ethic of the New Testament is to love our neighbor, and clearly included in this command are those who are, for whatever reason, attracted to the same sex rather than the opposite sex. We cannot use these five or six verses in the Bible to justify hatred or persecution; we cannot use any verses in the Bible to justify hatred toward anyone.

If people attracted to the same sex were to discipline their sexual thoughts and actions by God's power (just as a heterosexual must), it is difficult to say anything negative about their spirituality or Christianity in God's eyes. Some people are convinced that the biblical teaching on this subject is locked in the ancient world and does not apply to today. They should be very careful that they are not wrongly convinced. As Romans 14:22 says, "Blessed are those who have no reason to condemn themselves because of what they approve" (NRSV).

LIFE REFLECTIONS

Paul never quite gave us the tidy statement we want, namely, that God designed sex and marriage to be a blessing for life between one man and one woman. However, this summary encapsulates the various things Paul says about with whom you should and should not have sex, as well as the instructions about marriage. But Paul's own approach, particularly in 1 Corinthians 5–7, is much more practical.

He did not explicitly say marriage was designed to be between one man and one woman. But he did make it clear that he did not think a man should have sex with a man or a woman with a woman (Rom. 1:26–27; 1 Cor. 6:9). He assumed throughout his discussions of marriage that it was between one man and one woman, even though he never directly prohibited or addressed polygamy. Presumably it was not an issue in any of Paul's circles at the time.[5]

SEX DOES NOT EQUAL MARRIAGE

Paul had a similar approach to sex in 1 Corinthians 7, even if less edgy or stringent. The instructions he gave were to direct sexual desires away from inappropriate channels. He did not explicitly say, "Only have sex in marriage." He said in effect, "Do not have sex anywhere else." This distinction may seem small, but it has significant implications: It makes the act of sex less significant in itself than we often make it today. Some Christians almost equate sex with marriage to where, if a pair of teens stumble and have sex, they must get married because they are already married in God's eyes. Suffice it to say, a high percentage of such forced marriages, based on faulty ideals, end in disaster.

The New Testament knows no such view where the act of sex itself takes on such intrinsic significance. For Paul, it was not the act itself but the relational connection two people made in sex that was significant. Sex with a prostitute is a bad connection (see 1 Cor. 6:15); it infects the body of Christ. But Paul never suggested a person was married to the prostitute in God's eyes or the man needed to wait until all the other sexual partners of the prostitute died before he should then marry her (as if having sex with a person created a "married to" waiting list because the act of sex has taken place). Applying the sex-equals-marriage view to this situation yields such a bizarre and ludicrous result we see clearly how faulty it is. The Bible never makes a one-to-one connection between sex and marriage.

SEX IS NOT EXACTLY "ONE FLESH"

It is also important to distinguish between becoming one flesh with someone and having sex. True, the one implies the other—having sex with someone implies that you have become one flesh with them (see 1 Cor. 6:16). But if becoming one flesh with someone only meant having sex with them, Paul would scarcely have to remind the Corinthians that uniting with a prostitute implied becoming one flesh with her. Becoming one flesh implies a lifelong connection of identity that Jesus said was meant to be in marriage (Matt. 19:5–6). But becoming one flesh is bigger than sex, and it does not automatically imply a permanent relationship, as we saw in the case of a prostitute.

Just to make it clear how many false assumptions are often made in relation to becoming one flesh, consider Jacob's relationship with his two wives and two concubines (see Gen. 29:1—30:24). Jacob became one flesh with Rachel, and he became one flesh with Leah. He became one flesh with Zilpah, and he became one flesh with Bilhah. In short, a person becomes one flesh with every person he or she has sex with. Becoming one flesh does not necessarily imply a monogamous connection. Becoming one flesh does not in itself imply some intrinsic, permanent relationship with one person for the rest of your life. It would apply to a polygamous situation. It would apply to sex where a relationship should not continue. Sex is supposed to relate to a permanent relationship with one's spouse, but the New Testament does not treat failures as permanent connections.

REMARRIAGE AFTER DIVORCE DOES NOT EQUAL ADULTERY

In the past, some people have misinterpreted Matthew 5:32 to say that remarried people commit adultery with their new spouse every time they have sex. I knew of two people who each married young. The spouses of both had left them and remarried. Eventually, they married each other. When this couple celebrated their fiftieth wedding anniversary, some family members boycotted their celebration. They believed that the two were still married in God's eyes to the first person with whom they had sex, so they were committing adultery every time they had sex with their new spouse. Thus, they thought the couple had been living in adultery for fifty years. One person even suggested the perfect scenario might be for them to divorce each other and wait for the possibility to remarry their first spouses.

An innocent, but slightly skewed idea like sex equals marriage can have a devastating effect on people's lives. In this case, the Old Testament itself forbade a man who had remarried from ever going back to his first wife (Deut. 24:4). True, this prohibition also likely had much to do with its ancient context, but it clearly undermines the view that one remains married in God's eyes forever to the first person with whom he or she has sex.

In the end, Jesus' strange comment in Matthew 5:32 is typical of Jesus, speaking of plucking out eyes that cause you to sin (Mark 9:47) and camels going through eyes of needles (Mark 10:25). A man who divorced his wife was practically forcing her to marry someone else—how else would she survive? In effect, the man was forcing her to shame him by marrying another man, forcing her to commit adultery against himself (Matt. 5:32). Jesus' point was not to prohibit the woman from remarrying, but rather to shame the man who was divorcing her for selfish reasons. The woman would scarcely have had any say in the whole matter.

A man could not sleep with another man's wife. Paul also said a man could not sleep with another man or a prostitute. Since Paul assumed throughout 1 Corinthians 7 that a woman would be a virgin when she married, Paul forbade a man from sleeping with a virgin, who might easily be promised to someone already (1 Cor. 7:36–38). Such a situation might be what Paul had in mind in 1 Thessalonians 4:3–8, when he said not to wrong a brother with sexual immorality, although he might have been thinking of adultery.

So, the only other possible avenue for sex outside marriage for a man was sex with a widow. Here and in general, Paul set down a very basic principle: "It is better to marry than to be aflame with passion" (1 Cor. 7:9 NRSV). Paul thus effectively shut down every alternative route to sex other than within the context of marriage. Sex, a powerful force in life, must be carefully channeled. For this reason, Paul told husbands and wives to have sex regularly, so that they would not be tempted to seek it elsewhere (7:3–7).

THE VALUE OF LIFELONG MONOGAMY

It is hard to think of a force today that is more powerful than our sexuality. What we believe about sex and marriage is far from some theoretical or idealistic matter. It is the very stuff of our day-to-day lives. Sex makes and breaks marriages and families. And marriages not only have to do with the two key individuals involved, but also with children—humanity in its most vulnerable and damageable state. It is hard to think of another area of day-to-day life where one moment of self-gratification can have such lasting consequences.

The notion that marriage should be lifelong and monogamous is not some legalistic idea forced on society by dictatorial Christians or idealists. From the standpoint of contemporary values, it perhaps has more to do with giving our children a stable and nurturing setting in which to grow. In terms of the values of earlier generations, it had much to do with who owned land and the prevention of wars and feuds. While it may sound outdated to say so, it makes sense to see a correlation between the stability of a society and the stability of the relationships between people. And surely the marriage relationship is one of the most important, if not the most important, in society.

THE EXCEPTION LANDMINES

At the same time, it is all too easy to make these sorts of very important constants into unreasonable and oppressive rules without reasons, especially when it comes to exceptional situations. There are all sorts of landmines in making exceptions to rules. If a rule is valid, it is so because it is the best-case scenario. Refusing to allow for exceptions can unnecessarily destroy the lives of people, but so can making too many exceptions to valid norms.

Thus, there is the landmine of using exceptions as an opportunity for self-gratification. Surely, many of those who think they are the exception are not really. For example, surely every divorce involves a moral failure of some sort on someone's part. It may not be a sexual, moral failure, as in having an affair (physical or emotional). It may be a longstanding failure to be flexible or a chronic failure to value your spouse as much as you value yourself. It may be a cumulative failure to be willing to forgive the countless wrongs we all do unintentionally or intentionally to each other. Such failures build over time and can break our relationships, just as they can break our relationship with God.

The fact that we know people will wrongly take advantage of the exception clause leads some to close the door on exceptions altogether. This is understandable. But remember that no one fools God. It is often a lack of trust in God that leads us to want to make sure the person who is hiding behind an exception clause doesn't get away with it. But ultimately, this is God's business.

Another landmine in this discussion is the temptation to look for cultural loopholes in a desire to get out of obeying what the Bible says. Is not the Bible the Word of God for us as well as for them? We do not want to give an inappropriate loophole to those who would say the instructions of the Bible toward homosexual sex had to do with ancient cultural understandings of impurity to which we no longer subscribe. We do not want to give an inappropriate loophole to those who would say that since the Bible seems so un-explicit on premarital sex, we have to rethink the relationship between sex and marriage in the modern world.

However, we cannot ignore that the Bible was written for ancient audiences in ancient categories. We have to deal with it in context. The Bible was written first to them—it says so itself. The original audiences presumably understood the vast majority of what the biblical texts were saying. To suggest the contrary is inconceivable, especially since those who have studied the ancient world find regular and thorough parallels in the non-biblical literature and artifacts of those days.

The biblical books are clearly in dialog with the categories of their own contexts, and yet, our categories are often quite different from theirs. The commonality of all human thinking and the degree to which an action in one culture means the same thing in another are much smaller than many at first might imagine. This is especially the case for those who have not had much exposure to other cultures. The meanings of words and actions are more often different, rather than the same, when we compare the connotations today with the connotations then.

Again, most of these claims seem fundamentally beyond dispute. These basic factors all add up to the inescapable conclusion that the biblical teaching must be processed through some lens beyond the text, whether it be the lens of the Church, the lens of the Holy Spirit, or the rational lens of finding the points of continuity between that time and this time. Ideally, we would involve all three filters when appropriating the biblical text.

True, many people will try to use culture and exceptions as an excuse to get away with something they should not. Our desire to honor God by doing the right thing should lead us to take these potential factors into account. It is our desire to believe what is true, what God really thinks, that forces us to consider these elements in the equation. It is more comfortable simply to stick with a blanket rule or easy ideas on which we have never reflected, especially when we are not the ones having to deal with a potentially exceptional situation. It is more Christian to seek God's face prayerfully and corporately with hearts to do whatever God requires.

The Church today is thus forced to "work out [its] salvation with fear and trembling" on such issues (Phil. 2:12). We want it to be as easy as "God said it; I believe it; that settles it for me." But the reality is "God said it to them in a particular context; I believe it; that settled it for them." And we must, with fear and trembling, work together as the Church under the guidance of the Holy Spirit to join those instructions to them with what God wants to say to our world today.

FOR FURTHER REFLECTION

1. What, if anything, was surprising to you in this chapter? What ideas will you dig into a little deeper and pursue? Why?

2. What do you think the overall implication of Scripture is in relation to divorce and remarriage? When, if ever, do you think God allows for divorce? Remarriage after divorce? What is the position of your church or denomination on this issue?

3. What are your thoughts on those with homosexual desires who, by God's power, discipline their thoughts and actions? Can you think of any reason for considering them less righteous or saved than someone who, by God's power, disciplines their desires toward the opposite sex?

4. Which of Paul's teachings on the practice of sex seems timeless and universal to you? Are there any aspects of his teachings that you think relate primarily to his first-century context?

7

DISAGREEMENT
AND DISORDER

We first met the Corinthian church in chapter 5 where we saw that disunity was the fundamental problem in the community. This disunity showed itself in various factions in the church that thought they were superior to the others. Then, in the last chapter, we saw some of the problems the church had in relation to sexual matters. Some Gentile believers had apparently not changed their lifestyles of visiting prostitutes, and one had gone so far as to sleep with his step-mother. Meanwhile, it is possible that some women in the congregation were trying to use Christianity as an excuse to stop having sex with their husbands, perhaps even to divorce them.

In this chapter, let's look at the other issues the Corinthians were divided over. These largely fall into two categories: (1) questions over whether the Corinthians should eat meat that had been sacrificed at nearby temples to other gods, and (2) matters of Corinthian worship.

The second—problems in worship—seemed especially to bring out the divisions of the church, whether it be at the Lord's Supper, in how women dressed, or in the members' exercise of charismatic gifts.

DISPUTABLE MATTERS

At first glance, the question of whether one should eat meat sacrificed to a pagan god does not seem relevant to us today. There aren't a lot of pagan temples around these days, and I have never even seen an animal sacrifice. We might be tempted to think 1 Corinthians 8–10 do not relate to our world today.

PAUL'S GUIDANCE

If we step back, we can actually see in 1 Corinthians 8–10 some of the most relevant material in the New Testament to today. The reason is that these chapters deal with what we might call "disputable matters," issues over which Christians disagree. Christians—at least those in continuity with other Christians who have lived throughout the last two thousand years—agree on a lot of things. We agree on who Christ is and on the basic nature and power of God. We agree that Jesus rose from the dead and will come again. We agree that there will be a day of justice yet to come for the living and the dead. We agree it is important to live a life befitting God, one that is based on love for one's enemy and neighbor, and that murder, adultery, and all such actions are not acceptable to God.

But we have our own thoughts on countless additional issues, which some call *adiaphora* (Greek "indifferent things"), issues that are not part of the core Christian faith but that Christians disagree over. The problem is that Christians have historically sequestered themselves into their own little corners and vastly expanded the core faith. This is especially the case in America, where our democratic and entrepreneurial spirit has led to a proliferation of denominations. Inevitably, we come to see the ideas of our little group as those of God himself, which would not be too bad if we didn't go on to think of Christians in other groups as half-Christians and Samaritans.

It is here the debates at Corinth over food sacrificed at pagan temples are potentially some of the most important teaching in the New Testament on how to get along in the church when we disagree over things. As background, there were almost as many temples in the ancient world as there are churches in a typical American city today. All of these temples were involved in animal sacrifices. Ancient religion was not about how to live or how to treat one another. That was what philosophers talked about. It wasn't even about having a happy afterlife, since most of the ancients probably didn't believe in much of a personal afterlife.[1] Ancient religion was about keeping the gods happy so they didn't spew volcanic ash all over you or cause your boat to capsize at sea.

They sacrificed to the gods—a lot. Such sacrifices were not like the whole burnt offerings of the Jews, where the entire animal was consumed. Even in the case of the Jews, that was only one kind of sacrifice. Most sacrifices only burned off the fat to the god. The meat itself was then shared by the priests' families and the families of those who brought the sacrifice. Going to offer sacrifices could thus also be something like going out to eat at a restaurant, except you provided the meat. Some of the temples at Corinth even had rooms attached where people could eat, such as the temple of Asclepius, the god of healing.

Meat itself was the food of the rich. The vast majority of people in the ancient world did not have meat except on special occasions. A religious festival involved so much sacrifice that a poor person might have an opportunity to eat meat. Even on a normal day, there might have been enough animals sacrificed for some of the meat to end up in the marketplace.

It is here that the issue of conscience came into play. Likely, any meat one found in the public marketplace would have come from a nearby temple. This is food that had been dedicated to a pagan god.[2] A Jew in particular might immediately perceive a problem with the first commandment: "You shall have no other gods before me" (Ex. 20:3). Can a faithful Jew eat such meat and thereby not violate this central commandment?

As with so many issues today, most Jews did not see this question as debatable. Even James and the apostles of Jerusalem apparently did not see it as debatable. For them, this was a core issue, central to Christian Jewish faith.[3] The Jerusalem letter of Acts 15:23–29 forbade Gentile believers, in no uncertain terms, from eating meat offered to idols. This issue may have been part of the argument between Peter and Paul at Antioch, that Christian Jews could not eat with Gentile believers if they ate meat of uncertain origin (Gal. 2:12). John understood why the risen Jesus forbade blatant eating of meat that had been sacrificed to idols (Rev. 2:14).

However, it is possible that Apollos had not taken this approach in his teaching, although we have no way of knowing for sure. Most scholars believe 1 Corinthians 8 gives us some of the slogans the Corinthians used to justify not only eating meat sacrificed to idols, but also eating at those temples. They were saying things like, "no idol in the world really exists," "there is no God but one," and "all of us possess knowledge." They used that knowledge—that there really was no one home at the pagan temple—as a justification to boldly eat at such temples.

Their logic can be seen very clearly: I can eat boldly at a pagan temple because I know that its god does not really exist. Suffice it to say, this reasoning would not have gone over well in Jerusalem among the leaders of the Jerusalem church or among conservative Jews throughout the world. It is probably this issue alone that stands behind Daniel and other Jews not eating meat in Daniel 1:8. And we can see in 1 Corinthians 8–10 a certain squeamishness, even on Paul's part. It is one thing to eat meat in the marketplace, but actually to go and sit in a pagan temple was another thing.

Paul, with tact and consistency to basic principles, walked a fine line toward the issue both here and in Romans 14–15, giving us a great model for how we can get along together today when we disagree but feel very strongly about certain issues. Paul did not deny any of the Corinthian slogans. Yes, it is true that idols are nothing. Certainly there is only one God—and for us who believe, we might now add that there is only one Lord as well, Jesus Christ.[4]

Paul does not wish to contradict the strength of their conviction, of their knowledge. Scholars, especially in the 1700s and 1800s, used to resonate a little too much with Paul's affirmation of the Corinthians' knowledge here and the strong conscience of the person in Romans 14–15. The move toward monotheism was understood as part of the evolution of civilization, thus, it was all too easy to see this issue as one of "smart versus stupid," with Paul showing off his enlightenment.

So, when Paul said sacrifices at pagan temples were offered to demons (1 Cor. 10:20), those same scholars accused Paul of inconsistency, of saying that other gods do not exist in chapter 8, then affirming their existence in chapter 10. The problem is not with Paul, but with the biases of those interpreters. Paul was involved in a rhetorical enterprise here. He did not want to deny any of the fundamental principles of the Corinthians—or perhaps of Apollos. But he did associate pagan temples with evil spiritual powers.

His proposal was a compromise between the hard line position of Jerusalem and the liberated position of some Corinthians. First, it was simply a conflict of loyalties to go to a pagan temple. You were who you ate with, and you could not partake of both the table of demons and the table of Christ (1 Cor. 10:21). But meat in itself was neither clean nor unclean (Rom. 14:14; 1 Cor. 8:8)—a position with which the hard liners would almost certainly have disagreed. What was important was not the meat itself but what was going on in one's head while eating it.

Paul thus advocated a "don't ask; don't tell" policy. If one bought meat in the marketplace or if people offered food at their home, one could eat it without asking where it came from. After all, everything belonged (and still belongs) to God and so did that meat, regardless of where it came from. But if one found out it came from a nearby temple, he was not to eat it so that neither he nor those around him would see his eating as a conflict of loyalty.

LIFE REFLECTIONS

This incident potentially provides us with an incredibly helpful model for getting along with each other as Christians even though we disagree with one another. For one, we should accept the fact that we will disagree on various issues—even on issues we consider to be essential and core to Christian faith. That is to say, we will even disagree on which issues are actually disputable and which are not. The Jerusalem church likely did not agree with Paul's instructions to the Corinthians. They almost certainly thought it essential to find out where meat had come from before eating it, leading some Jews scattered throughout the world to become vegetarians (Rom. 14:2).

It is not difficult to find similar issues today. For some, it is how you baptize. For others, it is how you vote. Some who at least call themselves Christians believe monogamous, homosexual relationships are compatible with Christian faith. God knows what he requires despite our debates. Romans 14:22–23 give the final answer on Christian disagreements:

> The faith that you have, have as your own conviction before God.
> Blessed are those who have no reason to condemn themselves

because of what they approve. But those who have doubts are condemned if they eat, because they do not act from faith; for whatever does not proceed from faith is sin. (NRSV)

In other words, one may or may not be correct in his or her convictions, but at the very least, it is essential that a person act with the conviction he or she is being faithful to God.

Here is an essential point: We are not wrong to have convictions on what is core faith and what is not. But God is the final judge. It is not up to us to decide who will be in the kingdom and who will not. That is God's business. Christ commands us to love our enemies, so we must certainly love those who claim to be our brothers and sisters, even if we are not certain ourselves. The burden of proof is surely on those who stand outside historic Christian belief and practice; even if it is not to us they must prove themselves.

Interestingly, Paul did not associate evil with things themselves—the food itself was neither clean nor unclean.[5] This is a remarkable position for a faithful Jew, since the book of Leviticus clearly considers some foods unclean. Not just mainstream Jews, but no doubt many Christian Jews themselves would have disagreed with Mark's interpretation of Jesus' words in Mark 7:19—that Jesus was implying that all foods were now clean.[6] Despite Peter's vision in Acts 10, we find him wrestling with such issues years later in Galatians 2.

The key issue for the churches at Corinth and Rome was consideration of other brothers and sisters in Christ. When Paul called some strong and some weak, it is not entirely clear he was doing anything but stroking the egos of those who were causing dissension and strife in these communities. He was very tactful, beginning with where they were and leading them to the right course of action by way of skillful rhetoric. The fundamental principle was not to put any obstacle in the path of one's fellow believer that might lead him into sin or cause him to stumble. Here, as elsewhere in Paul's writings, the principle is to think of others before thinking of your own self-seeking desires.

It is thus no coincidence that Paul sandwiched 1 Corinthians 9 in the middle of his discussion of meat. In this chapter, Paul reinforced what he was asking the Corinthians to do by reminding them of how he surrendered his rights to their support and instead supported himself. He did not accept their patronage, as other traveling teachers like Apollos no doubt did.[7] Instead, Paul surrendered his rights for the betterment of the community. In like manner, he urged the Corinthians not to think of themselves or what they had coming to them, but to be willing to surrender their freedoms when those freedoms might harm another member of the community.

To be sure, there are plenty of issues where we might potentially anger someone else, but on which we are not in any danger of harming their faith. Paul was not telling us to do or not to do something because we might anger or offend someone else. We are talking about really harming someone else's faith here. On that point, Paul was quite clear. We should not exploit our rights in such a way that we hurt others.

In the end, Paul seemed to suspect some of the Corinthians of not really acting from faith in the first place. At the beginning of 1 Corinthians 10, he told of how the Israelites who left Egypt went on to worship other gods in the wilderness. They didn't make it, he eerily announced. He also indicated his place in the kingdom was not assured if he did not remain faithful (9:24–27).

Our takeaway is that we are to love our fellow believers, even when they disagree with us. Love and unity are far more important than agreement on every issue of belief and practice. Even when we feel as strongly as the Jerusalem church did about meat sacrificed to idols, we need to let God, in the end, make the final decision. After all, he will anyway.

THE LORD'S SUPPER

Chapters 11–14 of 1 Corinthians all seem to deal in one way or another with issues of worship in the church. Chapter 11 begins with the question of how women should dress in worship. It then ends with the shameful way the Corinthians are eating the Lord's Supper. Chapters 12–14 deal with the proper exercise of spiritual gifts, with the love chapter of 1 Corinthians 13 sandwiched in the middle of the discussion. It is a not-so-subtle reminder that unity is a "more excellent way" than arguing over who is spiritually superior (12:31 NRSV).

PAUL'S GUIDANCE

First Corinthians 11:17–34 just may have been one of the first parts of this letter Paul wrote. He mentioned that he had heard of divisions among them, and he partially believed it. Surely by this point in the letter, he is convinced! The ancients did not just sit down and write a letter the way we write an e-mail today. Writing a letter involved some expense and planning. It is possible that in the archaeological dig of 1 Corinthians, scholars have hit one of the earliest layers in this section.

The suggested social divisions that existed at Corinth seem especially to have come out in the way the Lord's Supper was eaten. Just as Jesus' Last Supper was a meal, so it would seem the earliest Christians observed the Lord's Supper as a meal. The "love feasts" mentioned in Jude 12 (the "agape") were probably their way of celebrating what we now call Communion or the Eucharist.

Eating in the ancient world was a big deal. People ate with those whose status was similar to their own or who might enhance their status. In Judaism, eating was a potential source of defilement because of the purity rules of Leviticus. Within this context, the Pharisees' concerns about Jesus eating with prostitutes and tax collectors were perfectly understandable.

The dysfunction of the Corinthian church during its love feasts flowed from the culture of the day and illustrated what the way of Christ was not supposed to be. It is not entirely clear from 1 Corinthians 11 whether everyone was expected to bring some food as in a potluck dinner or whether the host of the house, presumably Gaius, provided the bulk of the food. In any case, some believers apparently were getting to the meal later than others, presumably slaves and those of lower status. Meanwhile, the wealthy owner of the house and those of his social stratum had perhaps already feasted sumptuously and were drunk by the time the others have arrived.

Anticipating what will come later in his discussion of spiritual gifts, Paul criticized such individuals as not understanding the body of Christ. They thought themselves somehow more worthy than the others, when in fact, God does not deal in such distinctions. Some, Paul said, actually became sick and died as a result of their sin of division in the church.

LIFE REFLECTIONS

This passage in 1 Corinthians 11 has often led American Christians to become very introspective before Communion. They have taken the words, "Examine yourselves" (11:28 NRSV), to mean you need to have everything right with God before you take Communion. Some American Christians may even avoid the Sunday services that their church takes Communion out of fear. This passage actually has nothing to do with such hyper-introspection or the need to be completely right with God before partaking, as if one needs to mention and repent individually for every sin he or she has committed before he or she eats and drinks.

The Lord's Supper is actually an excellent time for us to hit the reset button on our relationship with God and Christ. But it should be celebrated with joy, not with dread or fear. The problem with the Corinthians was division and a divisive spirit, not individualized imperfection. Ironically, when we celebrate this communal meal today with individualized wafers and miniature cups, we usually miss one of Paul's main points—the unity of the body of Christ: "Because there is one bread, we who are many are one body, for we all partake of the one bread" (10:17 NRSV).

The Corinthians, as all the early Christians, likely had this meal every week, probably one of the most central activities they did together. Later, Christianity set the Eucharist off into a specialized ritual to be performed by specially-ordained priests. Very specialized theology developed around this tradition, centered on the words of Jesus at the original supper. Unless we want to say that God let Christianity wander off track for two thousand years, God apparently did not have too much of a problem with celebrating it this way. God surely meets each Christian tradition today in the way each has come to celebrate it. This is God's way, to meet us where we are, for we cannot possibly get to his level.

At the same time, many Christians could no doubt improve their celebration of the Lord's Supper by getting back to basics. Fellowship and the unity of the body of Christ are clearly the key dimensions of the meal in 1 Corinthians. Remembering and re-appropriating the sacrificial, new covenant-making death of Jesus is another obvious key function. Healthy Christian communities still find themselves accomplishing these functions in one way or another, as Christians regularly break bread together and set up mechanisms for accountability and thanksgiving to God and Christ. Communities not doing these things are deficient and unhealthy. The faith of someone who only comes to sit for an hour a week in a pew without fellowship or meaningful reflection on Christ can hardly be anything but anemic, if it can even remain genuine Christian faith for long.

WOMEN AND WORSHIP

For whatever reason, some of the women in the Corinthian church were a source of controversy. As noted earlier, some Corinthian women might have been trying to use the gospel as an opportunity to free themselves of their husbands and perhaps of sex. These same women may have been the focus of the first part of 1 Corinthians 11 and 14:34–35. Perhaps it is no coincidence that this is the only place in the letter where Paul mentions Aquila first and Priscilla second (16:19).[8]

PAUL'S GUIDANCE

In 1 Corinthians 11, the problem apparently had to do with conflict in the church from women not veiling their heads when the community worshiped together. Although scholars have debated quite a bit about the passage, it is believed the heart of the problem was married women not veiling their hair in the presence of men who were not their husbands.[9] Other Jewish literature from the same time period indicated pious, married, Jewish women wore a veil over their hair down to their shoulders (not a face veil). For example, in the Jewish novel *Joseph and Aseneth*, the widow Aseneth was told to put the veil of a virgin back on her head when she converted to Judaism.[10]

It is easy to imagine how this conflict might arise. Women would normally have worn the veil outside but not inside. Since worship took place in a home, though, they were faced with the question of whether to wear the veil. If the Corinthian church met in Gaius's house, as previously suggested in chapter 5, his wife and daughters might have resisted wearing a veil in their own home. In addition, scholars are not sure if Gentile women were in the practice of veiling. Perhaps some of these tensions were between Jewish and Gentile elements in the congregation, with

Jews finding temptation or offense in the absence of a veil.[11] So, while men and women who were not their wives were often kept separate, the house church put them in close quarters.

This hypothesis seems plausible, and it makes sense of what Paul said in the first part of 1 Corinthians 11. Paul affirmed the Corinthians for following the traditions he left them, but this chapter apparently qualifies the earlier instructions in some way. Since he went on to discuss proper relationships between husband and wife, the earlier instructions must have been something like Galatians 3:28, that in Christ there was not male and female.[12] In other words, the actions of the Corinthian women required Paul to qualify in some way the gospel's empowerment of women.

Paul invoked the cultural roles of husband and wife as they commonly played out in the Mediterranean world. Christians did not come up with the idea that the husband was the head of the wife, nor did it come from the Old Testament. The earliest use of this language is found in the Greek philosopher Aristotle in the 300s B.C. In his *Politics*, he suggested the husband is the head of the wife, and he rules over her in the same way the ruler of a city rules over the citizens of the city. He went on to say nature generally makes the male fitter to command than the female, although he acknowledged there were some departures from nature.[13]

So Paul invoked the cultural categories of his day to address apparent conflict taking place in worship because of men and women being in such close quarters in a home. He urged the wives of the assembly to wear their hair veils when they were praying and prophesying so they do not dishonor their heads, their husbands. An unveiled woman was like a woman with short hair, which everyone would have agreed was shameful. It made her look like a dishonorable woman, like a prostitute. It would be like taking off your wedding ring and flirting with other men, shaming your husband and possibly angering other wives who were wearing their rings.

Paul's talk of women appearing unveiled before God and angels raised the stakes even further. References to God as male are not literal but metaphorical to help human understanding. Nevertheless, God and angels were conceptualized as male. In fact, both Jews and Christians at the time understood Genesis 6:1 to be about angels having sex with human women, which is almost certainly to what 2 Peter 2:4 and Jude 6 are referring.[14] Like the men in their midst, Paul told women they should wear the veil on their heads as an indication of their honor in the presence of God and angels while praying or prophesying.

One point of great interest here is that Paul did not contest that women could pray and prophesy—which is the only preaching-like activity we hear of in the Corinthian church. Paul was trying to resolve conflict and remove disgrace in husband-wife relationships, but he assumed without question that women would be praying and prophesying in public worship in front of men. When we think of debates today over women in ministry, it is very important to notice Paul never connected the two issues. The language he occasionally invoked of husband headship has nothing to do with women ministering or preaching in worship.

This observation leads us to one of the two most controversial passages on women in the Bible: 1 Corinthians 14:34–35:

> Women should be silent in the churches. For they are not permitted to speak, but should be subordinate, as the law also says. If there is anything they desire to know, let them ask their husbands at home. For it is shameful for a woman to speak in church. (NRSV)

These are puzzling verses. Did not Paul already assume women could and did pray and prophesy in worship? For Paul to be consistent, we must assume Paul was not talking about spiritual speech but disruptive chatter. This verse thus has nothing to do with the question of women in ministry. Only one verse in the entire Bible, when read in context, seems to take a negative position on wives teaching their husbands, and I will address that verse in greater depth in the second volume.[15] In general, one should not base a practice on a single passage in the Bible, especially one as surprising and strange as 1 Timothy 2:12–15.

In the end, however, we would join the minority of scholars and conclude these verses were not likely to have been in the original copy of 1 Corinthians that Paul sent the Corinthians. Anyone who has used different versions like the NIV and the KJV will know these translations occasionally differ in text from one another. The reason is there are some variations among the thousands of copies of the New Testament that have survived from the ancient world. Evangelical scholars thus recognize some of the verses in the KJV were probably later additions absent from the first copies of the New Testament (see, for example, Mark 16:9–20).

In the case of 1 Corinthians 14:34–35, although these verses do appear in all the manuscripts we have, they do not always appear in the same place. Curiously, some manuscripts have them after verse 40 at the end of the chapter. A good explanation for this phenomenon is the suggestion that they were not originally in the text of 1 Corinthians but that they were written in the margin of a very early copy of the letter. Later copiers put them in the text at more than one place.

This is a slight manuscript basis for suggesting they were not original, but there are much stronger reasons for drawing this conclusion from internal evidence. The main one is that these verses do not fit here in 1 Corinthians 14. Paul was talking about the use of tongues and prophecy in worship. If these verses are not read, the train of thought is perfectly smooth:

For you can all prophesy one by one, so that all may learn and all be encouraged. And the spirits of prophets are subject to the prophets, for God is a God not of disorder but of peace. (As in all the churches of the saints . . . Or did the word of God originate with you? Or are you the only ones it has reached?) Anyone who claims to be a prophet, or to have spiritual powers, must acknowledge that what I am writing to you is a command of the Lord. (1 Cor. 14:31–33, 36–37 NRSV)

The two verses on women are unexpected and do not really fit the train of thought. But the nail in the coffin is the switch from the context of 1 Corinthians to a different context. First Corinthians addresses the church, singular, at Corinth (1 Cor. 1:2). It does not address churches, plural. But the two added verses tell the churches of God, plural, to make women keep silent. Because we as Christians read 1 Corinthians as Scripture, as God's word to us, plural, it is easy to miss this significant shift. But Paul was telling the singular church at Corinth to be orderly like the other churches of God. If he then went on to tell women to be silent in other churches, it would have left the Corinthians asking themselves, "Who is he talking to? Isn't this letter to us?" It is thus very unlikely that verses 34–35 were even in 1 Corinthians 14 in the first place.

LIFE REFLECTIONS

The issue of women in ministry is a strangely live one in the church today, ironically even in churches of my own denomination, the Wesleyan tradition. Wesleyans were ordaining women in the late 1800s, long before so-called liberal churches did and before feminism was popular. Wesleyans did so, along with many charismatic churches, because of our strong sense that the day of Pentecost implied women had the Spirit just as men and that Acts 2:17 was serious when it said the sons *and daughters* of those with the Spirit would now prophesy in the new age.

But it is deeply ironic that in an age when we recognize that there is nothing about a woman's brain that would imply she cannot lead or minister, Christians themselves are the ones holding out. In the New Testament, the empowerment of women is a major consequence of the new age, but it was tempered by the social conflict it caused at places like Corinth and perhaps Ephesus, the implied context of 1 Timothy. So then, full empowerment was limited by culture. Now, ironically, it is a certain segment of the church that is holding back full empowerment when Western culture would allow it.

In the end, we have to wonder if there are other things going on in the minds and hearts of those who will not let women answer any call God makes on their lives. And it is not always men who oppose women in ministry; it is just as often other women. If a person has sincere doubts, a great place to start is with the recognition that, even in the Old Testament, the tendency for men to take leadership was never absolute. There was always a place for exceptions like Deborah the general or Huldah the prophetess. If you are willing to make exceptions for those women who are truly called and not shut the door completely, then God will do the rest. You will see that God wants to call many women to all different levels of ministry and leadership in the church.

SPIRITUAL GIFTS AND WORSHIP

First Corinthians 12–14 forms yet another sequence of thought, this time on spiritual matters, principally spiritual gifts.[16] While chapter 12 treats spiritual gifts rather generally, Paul focused on two in particular in chapter 14—tongues and prophecy. Remember, the second half of

1 Corinthians addresses questions the Corinthians have sent to Paul. The first had to do with sex within marriage and whether virgins should marry. The second had to do with meat sacrificed to idols. Now, Paul addressed questions they had about spiritual gifts.

PAUL'S GUIDANCE

That Paul sandwiched a beautiful tribute to love in the middle of this discussion gives us a fair sense of the heart of the problem. Those with varying gifts in the community were not showing love and respect for the gifts of others but were instead thinking themselves superior because of the particular gifts they had. After going through various kinds of spiritual gifts a person might have, as well as key roles in the church like apostles, prophets, teachers, and so forth, Paul set love as a more excellent preoccupation than all the various gifts a person might have.

When he returned to his answer in chapter 14, Paul addressed the heart of the divisiveness. The entire tenor of 1 Corinthians 14 is to corral the practice of tongues speaking in Corinthian worship and to promote the practice of prophecy as more beneficial. "Pursue love and strive for the spiritual gifts, and especially that you may prophesy. For those who speak in a tongue do not speak to other people but to God; for nobody understands them, since they are speaking mysteries in the Spirit" (1 Cor. 14:1–2 NRSV). This correcting and steering the use of tongues continues throughout the chapter and suggests that it stood at the heart of their division over spiritual gifts.

It thus seems likely that some of the Corinthians thought of themselves as more spiritual than others in the church because they spoke in tongues. "If I speak in the tongues of mortals and of angels, but do not have love, I am a noisy gong or a clanging cymbal" (1 Cor. 13:1 NRSV), Paul told them. Speaking in tongues did not matter if you did not love others in the church.

Paul already chastised those who thought themselves spiritual back in 1 Corinthians 3:1: "I could not speak to you as spiritual people, but rather as people of the flesh, as infants in Christ" (NRSV). Just before this, Paul tried to distinguish what a spiritual person was like in contrast to a soulish person, sometimes translated as an unspiritual or natural person. We might even translate it as a merely animal person. Given the same use of the word *spiritual*, it is easy to see a connection with the question about spiritual matters in chapters 12–14.

This suggestion might seem strange at first—that those who "possess knowledge" in 8:1 (NRSV), who think they are already kings on earth in the kingdom (4:8)—are the same people as those who boast in their spiritual gift of tongues. Was this not the Apollos group, those who identified with the university professor from Alexandria? Was this not the group that knew "no idol in the world really exists" in distinction from the less intelligent people who were still superstitious?

Our Western perspective pushes us to distinguish intellectual, non-superstitious people who know there is only one God from emotional people who have mystic religious experiences and believe in demons and many gods. We are culturally programmed to think of people who speak in tongues as different from people who are intellectual. However, this way of categorizing people is modern, not ancient. Knowing God in the ancient world was an experiential kind of knowing rather than some Spock-like, dispassionate, intellectual pursuit. The philosophies of individuals like Pythagoras and Plato were deeply mystical and religious.

The speaking in tongues speaking at Corinth was apparently similar to some of the pagan religious experiences known in Greece. Paul started off chapter 12 talking about being "led astray to mute idols," a reference some scholars think is to the kind of wild, frenzied activity that went along with the festivals of Dionysus (12:2). In 14:23, Paul suggested an unbeliever coming into their meetings might think they were "out of [their] mind[s]," which might also refer to some of the ecstatic kinds of religious experiences that took place in the so-called mystery religions. Part of Paul's intention in these chapters was thus to avoid the appearance of pagan worship in the Christian assembly.

Whether or not this is the right reconstruction of the situation at Corinth, it seems clear enough that Paul's goal in 1 Corinthians 14 was to steer the use of tongues in worship in a healthy direction while not prohibiting its use. He began the chapter praising prophecy as good for the congregation in contrast to the self-edifying benefit of tongues. He mentioned briefly in verse 13 that a tongues-speaker should pray for the power to interpret their language; he then returned again for another twelve verses to speak of the barrier-creating effect of tongues on insider and visitor alike. Finally, Paul concluded with concrete rules for tongues and prophecy, with the stipulation that tongues were not to be used in worship unless an interpreter was present.

The entire tenor of the chapter was thus away from the use of tongues in public worship with the exception of those instances where an interpreter of the "languages" (the meaning of tongues) was present. This thrust was clear enough when Paul said tongues were not to be forbidden (14:39), which indicates that he had been limiting its practice but did not wish to eliminate it. A comment like, "I would like every one of you to speak in tongues" (14:5) is like the young woman who tells a young man interested in her, "I like you, but I don't want to date you." The first statement is meant to ease the pain of the second. So also, it would be great if they all spoke in tongues, but intelligible speech is really what is appropriate in worship. "I thank God that I speak in tongues more than all of you," Paul said to affirm the value of tongues. "*Nevertheless*, in church I would rather speak five words with my mind, in order to instruct others also, than ten thousand words in a tongue" (14:18 NRSV, emphasis added).

The rules that Paul laid down were to bring order to Corinthian worship. "All things should be done decently and in order" (14:40 NRSV). Two, or at the most, three, people should speak in tongues in any one worship time, and only if someone who had the gift to interpret was present. They should speak one at a time. The same applied to prophecy. As it was, Corinthian worship was chaotic: "When you come together, each one has a hymn, a lesson, a revelation, a tongue, or an interpretation" (14:26 NRSV).

LIFE REFLECTIONS

Since the beginning of the twentieth century, speaking in tongues has gained incredible prominence in Christian worship around the world. In fact, the fastest growing segment of Christianity in the world is the charismatic movement, particularly in the Southern Hemisphere. Some charismatic churches are careful to have interpretation of tongues speaking in worship; others are not. Clearly, speaking in tongues is, as Paul said two thousand years ago, edifying to the person who has the experience.

What is happening when a person speaks in tongues? Is it an angelic language? Is it a psychological phenomenon that some brains are simply wired to experience? Different individuals will no doubt have different opinions on these questions, and brain research might weigh in at some point with scientific evidence.

But what we know is that the experience is a blessing to the person so gifted, and we should rejoice with those who rejoice as fellow believers. Paul's concern that a worship service be uplifting to everyone present and not be a bad witness to outsiders who visit are concerns that should carry through to today. It may be, for example, that we have the benefit of so many different church options that those who attend tongues-speaking churches may actually find it uplifting to watch another believer speak in un-interpreted tongues. And such a church will rarely, if ever, be the sole representation of Christianity to the unbelievers in town. In other words, it may very well be the limitations Paul placed on tongues in worship that may not apply in some charismatic churches. By the same token, there may be some churches where the presence of tongues-speaking would be so divisive that Paul would have encouraged tongues-speakers there to practice their gift at home. The use of tongues in worship is not needed for the body and will only cause disorder. They can surrender their rights so as not to put a stumbling block in front of the church.

Are tongues today the same as tongues so long ago? After all, tongues-speaking seems to have been very rare in the two thousand years since the Corinthians till the Azusa street revivals of the early twentieth century. Some people would say that tongues were purely an early church phenomenon to spread the gospel at first to people who spoke other languages. But there is no clear biblical basis on which to claim such a thing.[17] It is true that the tongues speaking in Acts 2 seems to be other human languages, but the tongues speaking of 1 Corinthians 14 may very well be conceptualized as angelic languages (see 1 Cor. 13:1) or, at least, languages not known to the congregation.

Some people would say those who speak in tongues are serving as conduits for demons and often curse God in other languages. These stories are repeated with such a similar form that they are probably urban legends with little or no basis in fact. In general, it is dangerous to attribute to Satan what is actually the work of the Spirit. This is a sin Jesus says is unpardonable, so we should probably avoid such accusations (see Matt. 12:32).

Just as God often amplifies certain natural talents we have for ministry and Christian service, some people's brains may be wired to have this experience. After all, there are accounts of these sorts of experiences not only among Christians, but among other religious groups as well.[18] Perhaps God then sanctifies or amplifies this natural potentiality for such individuals, giving them a personal sense of blessing through the Holy Spirit. In any case, we cannot look down on this spiritual gift any more than we can think ourselves more spiritual than others for having it.

The lesson of the Corinthians is thus for the tongues-speaker—or in fact anyone with any special gift from God—not to think less of others in the community who do not have that gift. We are not more valuable to God because we have some particular gift. We may serve different functions in the body of Christ, but we are all of the same status, whether social or spiritual.

FOR FURTHER REFLECTION

1. What do you think of the idea that words, things, and actions become wrong primarily because of the way they are used, because of their context rather than because of any intrinsic significance they have? For example, how might it open you to seeing the world as something that God wants to redeem rather than the world as evil in itself? What implications does it bring to debates over whether Christians should celebrate Halloween or even Christmas because of previous pagan associations with those holidays?

2. What are some disputable matters today, things over which people who call themselves Christians disagree? How can Paul's treatment of food offered to idols help us navigate our way through such disagreements?

3. What is your takeaway from the Corinthians' problems with the Lord's Supper? How might it affect the way you take Communion next time?

4. How, if at all, has this chapter changed your thoughts on women both in the New Testament and today, especially when you take into account the first-century context of the New Testament? What might you do moving forward to advance the trajectory of the gospel in the church and home today?

5. How, if at all, has this chapter changed the way you look at tongues and spiritual gifts in the church? How might the way you relate to these sorts of practices change in the future?

8

MUTINY IN GALATIA

THE SETTING OF GALATIANS

Most scholars agree that Paul wrote 1 Corinthians while he was at Ephesus in the mid-50s. But with Galatians, there are significantly different theories about when, where, and to whom it was written. Until the twentieth century, the vast majority of interpreters thought this letter was written by Paul from Ephesus or even later in his missionary journeys. Scholars also thought Paul wrote it to the northern part of Roman Galatia, in the center of modern-day Turkey near Ancyra, the region where the ethnic Galatians had lived several centuries before Christ. But developments in our knowledge of Roman provinces have caused many scholars to place Galatians earlier in Paul's ministry and to a slightly different audience. In the mid-twentieth century, many evangelical scholars came to view it as the earliest of

Paul's letters, largely to work out some tensions between it and the book of Acts.

The Two Galatias

THE STANDARD EVANGELICAL INTERPRETATION

The position of most evangelicals, championed by F. F. Bruce, is that Galatians was the earliest of the letters Paul wrote, written perhaps from Antioch in about the year A.D. 48 to the churches he and Barnabas had founded on their first missionary journey.[1] Bruce's ingenious reconstruction is one that tidily cleans up a number of potential conundrums. In his scenario, Paul and Barnabas recently finished their trip to cities like Iconium, Lystra, Derbe, and a different Antioch in Asia Minor, in the south central part of what is now modern-day Turkey. We are now aware that this region was actually part of what the Romans called Galatia at the time, south Galatia.

In Bruce's reconstruction, the private meeting of Paul with Peter and James (Gal. 2:1–10) had taken place even before the first missionary journey. Bruce had observantly noticed that Paul had already gone up to

Jerusalem before that journey because of a revelation about a famine (Acts 11:30). So, Bruce speculated that the revelation that inspired Paul's visit to Jerusalem in Galatians 2:2 was the same revelation.[2] After all, both the visit in Galatians 2 and the visit in Acts 11 were described as Paul's second visit to Jerusalem.

In this scenario, before his first journey, Paul received private assurances from Peter and James that uncircumcised Gentiles could be Christians. But after the journey, he returned to continued controversy over the issue. The conflict came to a head when Paul and Peter had a knock-down-drag-out dispute at Antioch over whether Jewish and Gentile believers could eat together without the Jewish believers being defiled in terms of the holiness codes of Leviticus. James apparently pressured Peter not to eat with Gentiles, while Paul stood in front of the church and essentially called Peter a hypocrite.

Meanwhile, an already annoyed Paul heard that certain Christian Jews had infiltrated the very churches he and Barnabas had just founded (Iconium, Lystra, Derbe, and Pisidian Antioch). They were telling the Gentile believers that they needed to go all the way and fully convert to Judaism in order to be saved from God's coming wrath. Paul went ballistic.[3] He wrote to them in the strongest terms that works of Law like circumcision did nothing whatsoever to make them right with God.

The controversy finally reached such a fevered pitch that James and the leaders of the Jerusalem church called a meeting of all the key parties involved, the so-called Jerusalem Council or Jerusalem Conference of Acts 15. The key positions were heard. Certain Christian Pharisees presented their position (Acts 15:5). Peter championed the position that Gentiles would be saved by God's grace just as Jewish believers would (15:11). Barnabas and Paul shared stories of the Gentile conversions on their missionary journey.

Finally, James, the half-brother of Jesus, rendered a verdict. Gentiles did not need to be circumcised to be saved. But they did need to do four things: (1) They needed to stay away from things that came into contact with idols (like meat); (2) they needed to refrain from acts of sexual immorality; (3) they needed to drain the blood from animals rather than strangle them to death; and (4) they needed to stay away from blood in general.[4]

And thus, the conflict over Jewish and Gentile relations was largely settled, and Peter and Paul moved forward in unity and in common agreement on such issues. Scholars call this reconstruction of the setting of Galatians the "early South Galatian hypothesis," because it sees the letter written to the southern part of the Roman province of Galatia in about the year A.D. 48 just before a Jerusalem Council in A.D. 49. It creates a tidy scenario that accounts for some tensions between Galatians and Acts, while maintaining a harmonious and orderly picture of the progress of the early church. We therefore understand why it has been the most attractive reconstruction among evangelicals.

PROBLEMS WITH THE STANDARD EVANGELICAL APPROACH

Bruce's interpretation faces some problems on the details of Galatians, and it seems driven as much by ideological forces as by evidence. For this reason, most scholars in general have not adopted it. First, Bruce was almost certainly wrong to equate the "revelation" that led Paul to go up to Jerusalem somewhat privately (Gal. 2:2) with the revelation that led to the famine relief trip ("gift" trip) of Acts 11:30. The Acts 11 revelation had to do with the famine. The revelation Paul mentioned had to do with his understanding of salvation for the Gentiles.

Even more problematic is the timing. In order to make the timing work, Bruce had to take the expression "fourteen years later" not to mean fourteen years after Paul's previous visit, but fourteen years since he first experienced the risen Jesus.[5] Otherwise, Paul's visit in Galatians is pushed too late for the gift trip. But this interpretation is counterintuitive. Is not part of Paul's argument in Galatians 1 and 2 that he had not visited Jerusalem very often to derive his teaching from them, and that instead, he had received his understandings independently of them? Was not he saying it was three years after his conversion before he visited them the first time and then not again until fourteen years after that first visit?

This reading does present a minor tension with Acts, where the gift trip would have been an intervening visit. But there are many such tensions between the biblical accounts. Perhaps the best approach is to let them fall where they lie rather than insist on reconciling them all. When we try to reconcile them all, we often end up bending one or more of the texts to fit our reconstruction. We need to value and respect the text itself more than our desire to construct a plausible scenario that reconciles them all.

Attempting to harmonize the texts usually results in a reconstruction that fails to represent any of the texts. The text created by the interpreter is substituted for the original texts.[6] Nevertheless, it is possible to reconcile the natural reading of Galatians with Acts. Paul was talking in Galatians 2 primarily about visits having to do with theological matters, and it is conceivable that he might have omitted from such a list of visits one that involved no real interaction between him and the Jerusalem leaders on such issues.

In any case, the more likely timing of Galatians 2:1 puts Paul's visit to Jerusalem mentioned there at about the same time as the Jerusalem Council of Acts 15. Most scholars have thus concluded that the two events were one and the same. Paul presented the event as somewhat of a private meeting, while Acts presented the event as more of a public one. Here is the fundamental reason why many evangelicals have gone with Bruce: Acts 15 is different enough from Galatians 2 to require that one or the other be seen as a less straightforward historical presentation of the event.

But whether one thinks Galatians 2 was immediately before the Jerusalem Council or is a slightly different version of it, the timing places Galatians some time after the Jerusalem Council. What this means is that the meeting between Paul and James in Jerusalem, however it actually played out, did not resolve all the issues between Jews and Gentiles.

A third reason why the early dating of Galatians does not seem to fit the timeline of Galatians is that Paul mentioned in Galatians 4:13 that it was because of a weakness of his flesh that he preached to them the very first time. It is a relatively small argument, since it is possible we are reading too much into the word *first*. But the most natural way to take this Greek word is that Paul had already visited the Galatians more than once. If so, then Paul would not have written Galatians until at least after his second visit there, which was after the Jerusalem Conference.

AN ALTERNATE RECONSTRUCTION

Now, we reach the second reconstruction of the setting of Galatians. This reconstruction still suggests Paul wrote Galatians to the churches of South Galatia (Iconium, Lystra, Derbe, Pisidian Antioch), but that he did it at some point during his second or third missionary journey, either from Corinth or Ephesus. In this scenario, Peter took a trip north to Antioch after the Jerusalem Council, whatever its precise nature. For a time, he fellowshiped with Gentile Christians just as Paul and Barnabas did. Then James, nervous that their allowance to Gentiles would lead Jewish believers to be lax in their keeping of the Law, sent some people to check on what was going on at Antioch. These people convinced Peter and Barnabas they could not slack off on purity concerns just because the Gentiles could be saved without following them. Paul was upset, as in the other scenario.

There are two key differences in this scenario from the previous one. First, Paul seems to lose this argument. After all, he told us earlier in Galatians 2 that James, Peter, and John agreed with him on the issue of circumcision. If Peter and Barnabas had given in to his argument at Antioch, Paul would have told us in Galatians. The end result is that Paul's argument with Barnabas in Acts 15:39 was probably about more than just whether to take Mark along on their next trip. We remember that Acts, in keeping with its general approach, completely omits this controversy at Antioch. There is good reason to believe Paul left Antioch on somewhat tense, perhaps even bad, terms with the Jerusalem church. The tension is still evident when he returned to Jerusalem in Acts 21:20–22.

The second key difference involves the interpretation of the letter that Acts 15 described being sent as a result of the Jerusalem Conference. Its four prohibitions would actually solve the matter of Jew and Gentile believer eating together, at least in the minds of people like James, Peter, and Barnabas. If Gentiles would stay away from strangled meat with the blood still in it, from meat that had been sacrificed at a temple, and from sexual immorality, then Jewish believers could eat with Gentile believers. The early Galatians scenario was nice and neat on this question, because it considered the Antioch disagreement to have happened before the Council.

But if the argument at Antioch was after the Council, then the letter of Galatians seems a little anachronistic—at least if it is addressing the question of who you eat with.[7] Some scholars think it is giving bare bones requirements for Gentiles to be saved, in which case there would not be any real tension. But if it is telling Gentiles how they must get and prepare food in order that Jewish believers might eat with them, readers are forced to see Acts 15 as a somewhat abbreviated and creative presentation of a more complicated and drawn-out struggle in history.

In either case, it is clear that Paul did not agree with the letter's position. Paul neither mentioned the letter nor took its position when he dealt with the Corinthians on the subject of meat sacrificed to idols. One way or another, Paul's relationship with the Jerusalem church continued to involve some tension even into his second and third missionary journeys. And we see this fact in 1 Corinthians where Paul mentioned some at Corinth who said they "follow Peter" in a way that distinguished them from Paul (1 Cor. 1:12 NLT).

It was mentioned earlier that most scholars throughout Christian history assumed Galatians was written to north Galatia. I can only think of one substantial reason to maintain this position today. Paul said in Galatians 4:13, that he first preached the good news to the Galatians because of a physical problem. He went on to say how they would have been glad to give him their own eyes if they could have (4:15). Paul thus seemed to have been passing through some part of Galatia when he encountered eye problems that led him to change his plans for an extended period of time.

It is not obvious how this description of Paul's founding visit fits with the depiction of Paul's first missionary journey in Acts 13–14. South Galatia was hardly on the way between Cyprus and Antioch. To go there required intentionality on Paul's and Barnabas's part. To be sure, some scholars have questioned whether Paul took exactly this path historically. Some have even suggested that Paul might have been in Greece some ten years earlier than Acts depicts. But these reconstructions seem highly speculative. Readers really have no reason to question Acts' description of Paul's itinerary at this point. Someone might thus speculate that when Acts says Paul travelled "throughout the region of Phrygia and Galatia"

(16:6), he went to north Galatia and was held up because of physical problems there. For most of ancient times, only this area was actually called Galatia. The ethnic Galatians, although they were long gone by the time of Paul, had lived in this northern region.

However, the Romans expanded the territory in 25 B.C. to include the southern area. So, in Paul's day, the cities of south Galatia were considered part of Galatia as well. The New Testament provides no evidence that Paul founded churches in the northern territory, classic Galatia, while it mentions several churches Paul founded in the south. In addition, there is no obvious path out of south Galatia that would lead Paul some two hundred miles into north Galatia, which is in the middle of nowhere. Thus, it would seem south Galatia is the much more likely audience of Galatians.

Galatians was addressed to a Gentile audience who was being urged to convert fully to Judaism by undergoing circumcision. Those who were trying to convince them were most likely Christian Jews who came to Galatia from elsewhere, quite possibly from somewhere in Palestine like Antioch. It is important to recognize that their detractors claimed to be Christians, not Jews. They were like the Christian Pharisees of Acts 15:5. Paul would have probably considered them "false brothers" (see Gal. 2:4), but they thought of themselves as believers in Christ and the Jerusalem church likely would have as well.

The central issue of debate was circumcision. If the meeting we called the Jerusalem Council was widely known, it is a little strange that there were missionaries of a sort who were teaching the Gentiles should get circumcised.[8] But remember, Galatians 2:3 says Titus "was not compelled" (NRSV) to become circumcised, meaning it was still likely James and Peter's preference. It would thus be understandable if some were telling the Galatians they should fully commit and go the whole way.

One of the more peculiar features of the situation was the fact that these missionaries were apparently claiming that Paul himself agreed with them, or at least had submitted to the authority of Jerusalem. They were telling the Galatians that Paul himself thought it preferable for them to become circumcised (Gal. 5:11). How they made such an argument is puzzling, since Paul is strongly associated with the opposite position. Perhaps he and Barnabas were still somewhat tentative on the subject when they came through the area on the first missionary journey. After all, it was after the first journey that Paul made the visit of Galatians 2 to Jerusalem. Acts tells us Paul circumcised Timothy at Lystra on his second journey (Acts 16:3), which certainly could have given the impression that circumcision was the optimal scenario.

Whatever they specifically argued, the undermining of his mission clearly infuriated Paul. This situation was personal, and no doubt reminded him of losing the argument at Antioch. Now, they were tampering with his churches in his territory. One of the noticeable features of Galatians is that Paul did not offer thanksgiving at its opening, as in his other letters. Instead, he immediately chastised the Galatians for acting as if God's gracious acceptance of them was somehow not enough. They were beginning to observe aspects of the Jewish calendar (Gal. 4:10) and considering circumcision (5:2).

Paul's counterargument was not only that no amount of works of Law could make one right with God; he also argued that such Jewish particulars had no impact on one's status with God at all, particularly if one was a Gentile. To the Gentiles, God was offering a remarkable gift. Through the faithful death of Jesus the Messiah, he was offering both Jew and Gentile the possibility of being right with God, regardless of how much wrongdoing a person had previously done. To try, then, to earn God's favor by keeping the particulars of the Jewish Law was an insult, tantamount to a rejection of his grace.

The majority of scholars think that Paul might have been at Ephesus on his third missionary journey as he wrote Galatians, perhaps not too long after he wrote 1 Corinthians. But while many argue Paul's theology of getting right with God may have been intact very early on in his ministry, it does not really show itself in 1 Thessalonians and hardly at all in 1 Corinthians. But it is found after the time Paul wrote Galatians, especially in Romans. Other themes like "new creation" (Gal. 6:15; 2 Cor. 5:17) and the dangers of bad yeast leavening the body of Christ (Gal. 5:9; 1 Cor. 5:6–7) were also things Paul was thinking of during the time he was at Ephesus. Acts tells us that Paul rented out one Hall of Tyrannus while he was there (19:9). Is it possible that Paul ran a school of interpretation there? Is it possible that some of the arguments in Galatians are a product of his teaching in that hall? These suggestions are all speculation, but they are not impossible.

THE MESSAGE OF GALATIANS

The heart of the message of Galatians is about what constitutes right standing with God, either as a Jew or a Gentile, indicating a person is part of God's people.[9] The argument of Galatians is thick, perhaps the thickest in the whole Bible, but the basic point is that Jesus is the only path to be right with God. Getting circumcised or observing certain days in certain ways are irrelevant actions when it comes to a right standing before God. Trusting in what God has done through Jesus—that's the only way.

There are countless debates between scholars and churches over the details. Paul would no doubt be both perplexed and amused. It might be worth it to take a little time to spell out what Paul likely meant so we can avoid some of the arguments between Christian groups today over theology.

WORKS OF THE LAW

Paul said no matter how many works of Law a Jew might do, it would not make him or her right with God; and it will not justify. Five hundred years ago, Martin Luther interpreted what Paul said very generally—that no one could earn God's favor. No matter how many good works one did, he or she could not earn a right standing with God. Luther was correct. Paul did believe God's favor could not be earned (see Rom. 4:4–5). Whether Jew or Gentile, all had wronged God and others at some point (see Gal. 2:17; Rom. 3:23). In other words, we all need God's grace, his unmerited favor.

At the same time, Luther slightly changed the focus of Paul's argument. Particularly in Galatians, Paul was not really talking about faith versus good works in general. He was talking about whether works of Law, that is the Jewish Law, could gain you right standing before God.[10] In other words, things like circumcision, purity rules of Leviticus, and Sabbath observance were in the bubble above his head, not good works like feeding the poor or clothing the needy. One of the documents found among the Dead Sea Scrolls contains an argument over works of Law, and it discussed issues Jewish groups often squabbled over, like what makes a person unclean.[11] "Works of Law" did not refer to good works in general.

Therefore, Paul was primarily arguing over the parts of the Jewish Law that were most distinctly Jewish, the things that distinguished the Jews ethnically from other people. Around the world, people knew Jews did not eat pork or work on Saturday. These were exactly the kinds of works of Law that Paul targeted. These are the sorts of things at Antioch that got in the way of Jewish and Gentile believers eating together. Paul's main point in Galatians was that none of these things actually matter when it comes to right standing with God, particularly for Gentiles.

In fact, relying on such things can be a slap in Christ's face. God has offered a free gift through Christ's death on the cross. It is a gift so good, no one could possibly deserve it. Yet when you are insistent on trying to pay for it, you cannot accept the gift for what it is. Peter and James apparently agreed a person could not be in right standing with God apart from trusting in Jesus' death. Paul used a much-debated expression in Galatians 2:16, which implied that both he and Peter agreed on the fact that trust in the faithful death of Jesus on the cross was the only way to be right with God.[12] But where they disagreed was in the value of keeping the particulars of the Mosaic Law. Paul said those particulars did not help a person at all, while Peter and others thought that, at least for Jews, they still played a role in justification, in being pronounced right with God. Only trust in God and Christ can make you right with God.

THE EXAMPLE OF ABRAHAM

Paul used Abraham as his fundamental example of the principle of justification by faith. Abraham was a superb example because Paul could use him as a model for the justification of both Jews and Gentiles. Paul interpreted Genesis 15:6 to say that Abraham had faith in God, and God considered their relationship restored as a result of that faith (Gal. 3:6). Thus, Abraham was a model to Gentiles of how to be right with God. Those who have faith in what God did through Jesus Christ would be considered righteous by God, right with him. Paul understood God's promise in Genesis 12:3 that all the nations would be blessed through Abraham to mean they would be restored to God through faith, with Abraham as their example (Gal. 3:8–9, 14).

THE PURPOSE OF THE LAW

Paul's opponents no doubt had some arguments of their own, and most scholars think Paul was responding to some of them in Galatians. One of the key questions Paul needed to answer was what the purpose of the Jewish Law was. If it was not meant to show how to be in right relationship with God, then what was it for? Paul's answer was that the Law was like a child's guardian (Gal. 4:24) that watches over the child until it comes of age.

So also, the Law served several functions before Christ came. For example, it taught people the difference between right and wrong (see Rom. 7:7). Here, Paul shifted in what he was talking about. When he talked about works of Law, he seemed to be thinking of what many Christians thought of as the ritual or ceremonial parts of the Jewish Law.[13] But now he was talking about the heart of the Law, what later Christians would call the moral law. The fact that Paul could glide without notice between these various parts of the Jewish Law was the primary source of confusion over what exactly he meant.

Paul taught that before Christ, we were all under the power of sin in the world. Before Christ, the Law pointed out our weakness in the face of this power (see Gal. 4:3). But now that Christ has come, God's Holy Spirit is available to empower us to do what is right. We no longer need the instruction of our guardian, the Law. We have the power of the Spirit inside us to keep the essence of the (moral) Law.

FREEDOM FROM THE LAW

Paul's letter exhorted the Galatians not to let their freedom from works of Law lead to sinful living. This is the tightrope Paul's theology walked. He argued that the Jewish particulars of the Law could not make people right with God, nor were they able to live above sin before Christ. But Christ enabled them to receive the Spirit of adoption and sonship. If they walked in the Spirit, they would not fulfill the desires of the flesh (Gal. 5:16).

Today, as in Paul's time, works of law cannot make us right with God, but if we have the Spirit inside us, fruit will follow. The fruit of the Spirit are things like "love, joy, peace, patience, kindness, goodness, faithfulness, gentleness and self-control" (Gal. 5:22–23). Quite different are the works of the flesh: "sexual immorality, impurity and debauchery; idolatry and witchcraft; hatred, discord, jealousy, fits of rage, selfish ambition, dissensions, factions and envy; drunkenness, orgies, and the like" (5:19–21).

As Paul closed his letter to the Galatians, he pointed out the hypocrisy of those urging them to get circumcised. They were not models of keeping the Jewish Law. Paul knew, since he was once a Pharisee who paid close attention to such things. In the end, it was neither circumcision nor uncircumcision that mattered before God, he claimed. It was, and is today, the new creation of the Spirit made possible through the cross of Jesus the Messiah.

LIFE REFLECTIONS

Those who apply the book of Galatians often jump immediately to the freedom we have in Christ from the oppression of our sin and failure. We do not have to worry about being good enough or smart enough because God likes us. Certainly, there is a lot of truth to these applications. We should be immensely grateful for "a gracious and compassionate God, slow to anger and abounding in love" (Jon. 4:2). As Paul said, quoting Psalm 32, "Blessed are those whose iniquities are forgiven, and whose sins are covered; blessed is the one against whom the Lord will not reckon sin" (Rom. 4:7–8 NRSV).

GOOD WORKS VS. LEGALISM

At the same time, this teaching has often been presented in incorrect and unhelpful ways. For example, Paul has often been pitted against a legalistic Judaism that believed you had to earn your right status with God. Against this idea of "works-righteousness," some say, Paul came with the revelation that one cannot be saved by good works, but by faith alone. Similarly, Martin Luther is championed by Protestants as setting the Roman Catholic Church straight, where he, like Paul, recognized the truth of justification by faith alone, while the Catholics believed good works were necessary for salvation.

Again, there is some truth to these scenarios, although they do skew history a little. For example, Jewish literature from the ancient world generally shows that Jews also believed it was only the grace of God that made a good relationship with God possible for them. They put a high premium on living a righteous life in response to God's grace, but so does the New Testament if we are willing to listen to it.[14] The main difference is the centrality of Christ in procuring God's favor and the way Paul emphasized the Holy Spirit as how one was empowered to live that righteous life.

The Roman Catholic Church has also dialogued significantly with the Lutheran Church in recent years and has acknowledged justification is first and foremost on the basis of faith.[15] But it also insists good works must follow for final salvation. When we get to 2 Corinthians in chapter 10 and then later come to Romans in the second volume, we will find that Paul himself said some similar things. Paul never actually used the expression "justification by faith alone." That phrase comes rather from Martin Luther.[16]

Galatians does carry a warning against legalism. Legalism is not a matter of being conservative or being strict in your lifestyle. Legalism is an attitude that enjoys rules for their own sake and puts rules above the people they are meant to benefit. If Paul seems inconsistent here, it is because he knew what God wanted but brought different arguments at different times to get his audiences there. He knew the Gentiles could be in by faith. He knew that Jewish and Gentile Christian should eat together. And he wrestled to show these truths in the different situations addressed by the arguments of his letters.[17]

One way we might summarize Paul's argument here is that people trump the rules, even sometimes the rules of Scripture. What drove the argument between Paul and Peter at Antioch was how to play out the purity regulations of Leviticus. But the rule of the unity of Christians required that exceptions be made to those rules. Galatians 4:9 seems to shockingly equate keeping the Jewish Law with enslavement to evil spiritual forces that hold power over the basic elements of the world.

USING SCRIPTURE APPROPRIATELY

Paul was an apostle, and we are not, but he showed at times a shocking liberty in the way he reinterpreted Scripture to counteract his opponents. One of the most striking is his allegorical interpretation of Sarah and Hagar, the wife and concubine of Abraham respectively. Perhaps his opponents had used them as a parable of Jew and Gentile. Paul countered by allegorically comparing Sarah the heavenly Jerusalem with Hagar the earthly one. Those who put too much primacy on the earthly city were enslaved like Hagar, while those who were part of the heavenly Jerusalem were free like Sarah (see Gal. 4:21–31).

Galatians is thus more than a reminder that God does not strictly judge us on how good we are but on our willingness to trust in his mercy. It is a reminder that, in our attempt to serve God, we can subtly find ourselves using Scripture and our traditions to undermine God's more fundamental purposes. The fundamentalist interpreters of the early 1800s seemed to have great biblical arguments why slavery was a perfectly legitimate Christian institution. Do not the household codes of Colossians and

1 Peter assume slavery and tell slaves to obey their masters? It was those, like Paul, who could see the more fundamental spiritual principles—more central than random verses—who pushed back against slavery. And so, we have moved closer to the kingdom.

A similar battle is currently in play between those who believe God might call women to play any role in the church or the home. Once again, some will continue to point to verses in the household codes or in 1 Timothy. But the church as a whole will move forward, following the more fundamental principle that "in Christ there is not male and female" (Gal. 3:28, my translation).

FREEDOM NOT TO SIN

Another key principle is the importance of not allowing one's freedom to become an opportunity for sin. Galatians 5:16 is quite stark: "Walk in the Spirit and you certainly will not fulfill the desires of the flesh" (my translation). Here we find no pessimism of regular moral failure, no sense of sinning every day in word, thought, and deed. What we find instead is an optimism of the Spirit's power, that if we will only open ourselves up to the empowerment of the Spirit, we will find the fruit of the Spirit permeating our lives.

FOR FURTHER REFLECTION

1. What difference, if any, would you say decisions about the date and location of Galatians would make to you, aside from knowing? How would your decision one way or another make a difference to your understanding of Paul, this letter, or anything else?

2. What do you think the phrase "justification by faith" means? How would you say a person comes to be in right standing with God?

3. What do you make of Paul's statement that a person who walks in the Spirit will not fulfill the desires of their sinful flesh?

4. Have you ever inappropriately put earthly rules above the command to love others? Can you think of any of those rules that should trump acting lovingly toward others?

JOY IN THE
FACE OF DEATH

Four of the Pauline letters in the New Testament hint that they were written while Paul was in prison: Ephesians, Philippians, Colossians, and Philemon.[1] Traditionally, Christians thought Paul wrote these from Rome while he was waiting to appear before the emperor Nero (see Acts 28:30–31). But none of them actually say where Paul was imprisoned when he wrote them, so, various scholars have suggested other places of origin, like Caesarea in Palestine or Ephesus in Asia Minor.

IMPRISONED AT EPHESUS?

When thinking about these letters, it is important to realize that prison was not usually a punishment in the ancient world. Rather, a person went to prison as they waited to appear before the appropriate official. Punishment was dispensed immediately after a verdict was reached and was usually death, exile, or fines. While people waited for their appearance, they would have to find someone on the outside to provide them with food and other necessities.

The book of Acts only tells of two imprisonments Paul experienced of any length: (1) about two years in Caesarea after he was arrested in Jerusalem (ca. A.D. 58–60), and (2) about two years under house arrest in Rome (ca. A.D. 60–62). Acts also mentions an overnight stint in Philippi (16:23–39), and the possibility cannot be ruled out that he spent a day or two in Corinth before he appeared before the Roman governor Gallio (Acts 18:12–17). Although it cannot be determined for certain how many times Paul was imprisoned, it is possible that he was in jail a few more times than Acts mentions.

In particular, many scholars suggest Paul might have been imprisoned at some point during the three years he was at Ephesus. Others strongly resist this idea because Acts does not tell us of any imprisonment during that period. But it does tell of a rather serious incident at the end of Paul's stay at Ephesus in which a mob riot was involved. At this point, Acts merely says Paul left Ephesus "after the uproar had ceased" (20:1 NRSV). Those who see Acts as an almost documentary-style report find it hard to believe that it would have failed to tell if Paul had been arrested because of this event.

Nevertheless, there are good reasons to think Acts is presenting the story with creative artistry and emphasizing some things in a way that leads it to omit others. For example, in the incident where they lowered Paul down the wall of Damascus in a basket, Acts only says that the Jews were plotting to kill him (9:23). We only learn from Paul himself that it was the Arab governor in the city, possibly under orders from King Aretas, who was trying to arrest him (2 Cor. 11:32). This was after a three-year period involving some time spent in Arabia

(Gal. 1:17–18)—likely in Aretas' kingdom. Acts tells us nothing about this incident. This is only one instance, but it may reflect a tendency on Acts' part to de-emphasize conflicts between the early Christians and Roman authorities and to emphasize the Jews as Paul's primary troublemakers.

Paul's own writings give us hints of at least one run in with the Romans at Ephesus, and possibly two. As early as 1 Corinthians, he mentioned having fought with "wild beasts" there at Ephesus (15:32). This statement should not be taken literally because Paul presumably would have died. The most likely meaning is that Paul had some significant altercation with the Roman authorities early in his stay at Ephesus.

Paul alluded to an even more serious encounter with authorities around the time of the riot. In 2 Corinthians, just after he left Ephesus, Paul spoke of "the affliction we experienced in Asia; for we were so utterly, unbearably crushed that we despaired of life itself. Indeed, we felt we had received the sentence of death" (1:8–9 NRSV). This sentiment seems stronger than merely being afraid he would be killed in a riot. It sounds more like Philippians 1, where Paul was hard pressed in his imprisonment to know whether he would rather have a verdict of death and go to be with Christ or whether it would be better for him to be acquitted (1:21–24).

While it is possible Paul wrote all four of his "Prison Epistles" from Rome, he may have written some of them while imprisoned at Ephesus waiting to appear before the Roman governor. I have decided to treat Philippians in this volume and the other three prison letters in the next (Philemon, Colossians, and Ephesians). Paul may not have written Philemon from Rome, but it is much easier to grasp the messages of these three books if I treat them all together from a vantage point at the end of Paul's life. Similarly, Paul might have written Philippians from Rome, but it fits much better with what is known if he wrote it from Ephesus.

THE END OF PAUL'S STAY AT EPHESUS

I quoted 2 Corinthians 1:8 above, where Paul said he had felt a "sentence of death" (NRSV) hanging over his head in his final days at Ephesus. Acts tells us about a silversmith named Demetrius who made shrines to the goddess Artemis (19:24). The temple of Artemis at Ephesus was one of the Seven Wonders of the Ancient World, and you can still see a few of its pillars if you visit the ruins of the city. Acts says Demetrius stirred up the guild of idol makers, who began to shout, "Great is Artemis of the Ephesians" (19:28) until the city was in chaos. They actually dragged some of Paul's coworkers into the theatre (which you also can still see today).

The theater at Ephesus mentioned in Acts 19:29.

Although Acts says nothing of Demetrius bringing charges against Paul, it does mention that the city clerk brought up the possibility (19:38). Perhaps Acts is hinting that Demetrius did bring Paul up on charges, and that Paul was imprisoned there at Ephesus to await trial for a significant amount of time. If so, it may have been during this time that Paul wrote Philippians, one of his most precious letters—and one in which he seemed most humbled by his circumstances. Is it any surprise that, when Paul passed back through Asia, he did not stop at Ephesus, but met with its elders south of the city, in Miletus (Acts 20:16)? They came to him, and he avoided the city.

The tone of Philippians fits such an uncertain time.

For to me, living is Christ and dying is gain. If I am to live in the flesh, that means fruitful labor for me; and I do not know which I prefer. I am hard pressed between the two: my desire is to depart and be with Christ, for that is far better; but to remain in the flesh is more necessary for you. (1:21–24 NRSV)

This fits the tone of what Paul said of his final days in Ephesus:

We do not want you to be unaware, brothers and sisters, of the affliction we experienced in Asia; for we were so utterly, unbearably crushed that we despaired of life itself. Indeed, we felt that we had received the sentence of death so that we would rely not on ourselves but on God who raises the dead. (2 Cor. 1:8–9 NRSV)

The logistics of Philippians also fit Ephesus better than Rome. For example, Philippians implies news has gone back and forth between Rome and Ephesus at least four times between Paul's arrest and his writing of the letter: (1) news reached the Philippians of Paul's imprisonment;

(2) they sent resources for him by way of a man named Epaphroditus; (3) Epaphroditus became ill and news of his sickness reached the Philippians; and (4) news of the Philippians' reaction to the illness of Epaphroditus travelled back to Paul. Certainly, Paul was imprisoned long enough at Rome for news to travel back and forth this many times, even though each trip would take well over month, probably closer to two. But this back and forth would happen much more naturally between Philippi and Ephesus, perhaps only a little more than a week apart each way.

Paul also expressed confidence that he would ultimately be released (Phil. 1:25) and expected to then visit Philippi (2:24). He planned to send Timothy ahead with news of the outcome of his trial (2:23). Then, when Timothy returned, Paul hoped he himself would go (2:19, 24). This is, again, quite a distance to wait for Timothy to get to Philippi and back from Rome. It makes much more sense if Timothy was leaving from Ephesus.

Acts records Paul going to Philippi after leaving Ephesus (Acts 20:1–2). Meanwhile, Romans 15:23 says Paul had no intention of ministering anymore in the east when he left the region. He had his sights set on going even further west to Spain (15:24). If Paul was writing Philippians from Rome and thinking of going back east, he had changed his plans significantly from when he had left the area.[2]

Mention of the imperial guard (Phil. 1:13) and of Caesar's household (4:22) has easily given the impression that Paul was writing from Rome. But Ephesus was the capital of the Roman province of Asia and so had a Roman proconsul seated there. This Roman governor would also have imperial soldiers, and the entire administration of the Roman Empire everywhere was part of Caesar's household, since a household included servants and all who served the "house."[3] While these agents of Caesar would certainly be present in Rome, they were also present in Ephesus.

While Paul could have written Philippians while imprisoned at Rome, Ephesus seems to fit the particulars of the letter as well or better. The main reason not to adopt this scenario remains one's sense of how much creativity and selection Acts employs. A quick comparison of Luke with Mark probably suffices to show Luke was not simply a passive chronographer.[4]

It seems likely, then, that at the end of Paul's stay at Ephesus, one of the metalworkers of the city brought charges against him, resulting in a prolonged imprisonment as Paul waited to appear before the Roman proconsul.

The letter indicates a strong and warm relationship between Paul and the church at Philippi, better than with any other church it would seem. Even when Paul first left Philippi, the Philippians had sent material support to him more than once when he was in nearby Thessalonica (Phil. 4:16). So it was natural that they would send similar aid to Paul when he became imprisoned at Ephesus. Paul was grateful for their help, but he also did not want them to think he was dependent on it. He did not want the strings that usually came with receiving patronage.

In good, Stoic fashion, Paul told them he had learned to be content both when he had much and when he had little (Phil. 4:12). In all circumstances, it was God who gave him strength to do what needed to be done (4:13). And, it was God who would supply all their needs as well (4:19). Philippians is thus one of the most encouraging books in the New Testament. It was written in the context of persecution and suffering (see 1:29), but one of its most prominent themes is rejoicing (1:18; 3:1; 4:4). If Paul could rejoice because of the strength given him from the Lord, even though he was potentially facing a death verdict, then we can too, whatever our circumstances.

LIVING WORTHY OF THE GOSPEL

The key verse of Philippians seems to be 1:27. After Paul greeted the Philippians (1:1–2) and after he thanked God for them and rehearsed some of his current situation (1:3–26), he began the body of the letter with an admonition for the people to "live [their lives] in a manner worthy of the gospel of Christ" (1:27 NRSV). Most of the remaining letter plays out this general instruction.

Perhaps the main goal Paul had in mind was for the Philippian church to be unified and loving toward one another, both in the face of opposition and in terms of tension among themselves. Just after he told them to live worthy lives, he said he wanted to hear that they were "standing firm in one spirit, striving side by side with one mind for the faith of the gospel" (1:27 NRSV). He wanted them to be "of the same mind, having the same love, being in full accord and of one mind" (2:2 NRSV). He wanted them to look out not only for themselves but for others as well (2:4) and not to operate "out of selfish ambition" (2:3).

Near the end of the letter, Paul specifically called out two women who worked together with him when he was at Philippi: Euodia and Syntyche (4:2). As he earlier encouraged the entire assembly, he urged them in particular to "be of the same mind in the Lord" (NRSV). These two had struggled beside Paul in the work of the gospel, along with someone named Clement and, perhaps, Epaphroditus.[5] But somewhere along the way, they had come into conflict. As he had with the Corinthians, Paul urged the Philippians to heal the disunity among them.

The most majestic part of Philippians is the so-called "Philippian hymn" of 2:6–11.[6] Paul used the example of Christ's selfless suffering for others as a model for how the Philippians should behave toward one another (2:5). It is not certain whether Christians somewhere actually sung these words. The rhythm of the words is not entirely clear and the lines are not all the same in length. Most scholars think, wherever the poem originated, Paul interrupted it at some points with commentary. Would a group used to singing such words not have been irritated at having the flow of a hymn interrupted?[7]

Nevertheless, the words do have a rhythm, and the early Christians did compose and use hymns in their worship (see 1 Cor. 14:26). The hymn seems to fall into three parts of four lines each, with Paul expanding on a few points. The places where Paul might have added to the hymn are in parentheses. The translation is my own:

> Although he existed in the form of God,
> He considered equality with God not something to exploit,
> But he emptied himself,
> Having taken the form of a servant.

> Having become in the likeness of mortals,
> And having been found in shape as a mortal,
> He humbled himself,
> Having become obedient to the point of death
> (even death on a cross).

> Therefore, God even super-exalted him,
> And graced on him the Name above every name,
> That (at the name of Jesus) every knee should bow (whether in heaven or on earth or under the earth) and tongue confess,
> That Jesus Christ is Lord (to the glory of God the Father).

This reconstruction, like all of them, is not without its problems, leading some simply to abandon the notion that there is even a poem here. Many scholars are content to suggest Paul simply waxed somewhat poetic on the spot. The rhythm of the last stanza above in particular is difficult and different from the first two, which have a much clearer poetic structure. Nevertheless, the poem seems to have enough rhythm with apparent interruptions to suggest that Paul is drawing it from somewhere else.

Several features of the hymn are quite remarkable. Most scholars take the first stanza to be about Jesus' pre-existence before he assumed human form.[8] Yet the most remarkable part of the hymn is in the third stanza where God gives to Jesus the "name that is above every name" (2:9). This name can hardly be anything but a reference to Yahweh, the very name of God. Yahweh was translated into Greek as "Lord," and so the name God bestowed on Jesus at the point of his resurrection was surely "Lord," not Jesus. The hymn thus sees Jesus receiving the very name of God as God raises Jesus from the dead and super-exalts him to his right hand.

Paul used this hymn about Christ to show the Philippians both the attitude they should have and, perhaps, what the ultimate benefit of such an attitude is. First, Jesus was none other than the Son of God, a status of royalty and kingship that none of them had. Even with such a high status, Jesus did not use his divine status for his own advantage. Rather, he assumed the status of a servant. And once he had assumed the shape of a mortal, even though he looked like any other human being, he humbled himself even further—he endured the most shameful form of capital punishment in use at the time: crucifixion.

It was to these lengths of service and sacrifice that Paul called the Philippians, urging them to embrace the interests of others. In the case of the hymn, God seems to have exalted Jesus even higher than he had been before. If he had been in the form of God before, now he was super-exalted with the very name of Yahweh. So also, perhaps Paul meant to imply, the Philippians would eventually be exalted by God if they would be servants then.

The final chapter of Philippians is filled with other items regarding living as citizens of heaven (1:27; 3:20).[9] Their true citizenship was not on earth, tied up with any earthly city or empire. Paul told them not to be anxious about anything but to rely on God (4:6). He told them to let others see how gentle they were (4:5). He encouraged them to think about noble and uplifting things (4:8). Throughout, he had a mellow spirit. His ordeal had humbled him, and the same spirit can be seen in 2 Corinthians 1–9, which is dated to soon after Paul wrote Philippians.

PAUL'S RÉSUMÉ

In the middle of Paul's exhortations to rejoice in suffering and to have a servant attitude like Christ's, we suddenly find Paul warning the Philippians about Judaizers, those who would insist the Philippians needed to be circumcised to be saved. The change in subject is so unexpected that some scholars have even suggested Philippians 3 came from another letter Paul wrote to the Philippians. There is probably not enough evidence to warrant such speculation, although it is possible. Nevertheless, assuming Paul had recently written Galatians, it makes sense he would have had these Judaizers in mind and would want to warn others in case they came to town.

Paul suddenly changed subjects and warned the Philippians to "Beware of the dogs, beware of the evil workers, beware of those who mutilate the flesh!" (3:2 NRSV). His language was deeply ironic, since a Jew might just as well refer to a non-Jew as an uncircumcised dog. Paul turned the tables and suggested that his enemies were the truly uncircumcised ones—their hearts were uncircumcised (see Rom. 2:28–29). They thus were not the true "circumcision" (*peritome*); they were not truly set apart as God's people. They are the "mutilation" (*katatome*), bent on getting Gentile believers to convert fully to Judaism and more interested in cutting flesh than in changing hearts.

Some scholars debate whether Paul was referring in these comments to non-believing or to Christian Jews. It seems that, as in Galatians and 2 Corinthians 10–13, Paul was referring to other believers rather than to non-believing Jews in general. Since, it seems that, he had very recently written Galatians, he was concerned that his ministry to Gentiles not be undermined elsewhere as well. He was concerned his detractors might try to convince his churches to establish "a righteousness of [their] own that comes from the law" instead of a "righteousness that comes from God and is by faith" (Phil. 3:9).

But Paul also wanted to make it clear that his Jewish credentials were impeccable, in fact, better than those of his opponents. He was circumcised the eighth day of his life like they were (3:5). He spoke Aramaic as a first language and could read the Bible in the original Hebrew (3:5). Before he believed, he was a zealous Pharisee, like some of the strictest of all believers in Jerusalem (see Acts 15:5). As far as righteousness based on Law-keeping went, he was blameless (Phil. 3:6).

Thus, Paul was not like his opponents at Galatia, who did not even keep the Law themselves (Gal. 6:13). He had kept the Law as well as it could be kept. To see Peter and Barnabas feebly remove themselves from eating with Gentiles at Antioch over issues of purity must have been a joke to Paul. After all, he had really kept the Law. They had never kept the Law as well as he did (see Gal. 2:14). Paul did not say he had been a miserable failure before believing. He just indicated Law-keeping was not what God was looking for. What God was (and still is) looking for was so incredible, these sorts of things paled in comparison.

What God looks at is the faithful death of Jesus Christ on the cross, the faith of Jesus Christ (3:9, my translation). To participate in Christ's death through baptism (see Rom. 6:3–4) and to share in his sufferings is to look forward to a share in his resurrection as well (Phil. 3:10–11). All of Paul's past accomplishments and credentials as a faithful Jew are like rubbish when placed next to the excellence of what being in Christ offers.

Paul suggested he was not yet guaranteed this resurrection of the dead (Phil. 3:11–12). He had not yet been perfected in this way, the perfection that would happen when the dead were raised. But he needed to continue throughout his life to pursue that goal and that prize, the prize of the heavenly call of the resurrection (3:14), as we must today. We must continue to live a life worthy of the gospel (2:27), we must work out together our way to final salvation (2:12), knowing that God is inside and among us, working in us to bring his will and his good pleasure to pass (2:13). If we are faithful by God's power, then one day God "will transform the body of our humiliation that it may be conformed to the body of his glory" (3:21 NRSV).

This is not the way 3:12–15 are usually interpreted. "Not that I have already obtained this" (3:12) is usually taken to mean absolute perfection—Paul had not yet reached absolute perfection; he was striving toward it. But Paul wasn't talking about absolute perfection. What he said he was striving to attain in the previous verse was the resurrection from the dead (3:11) or, as he went on to call it, the "heavenly call" (3:14 NRSV). This was the perfection he did not yet have. These verses are thus no excuse for complacency in our current imperfection. Paul's expectations of the believer were much higher than most of ours are today.

LIFE REFLECTIONS

Philippians, like 1 Corinthians, seems to easily bridge the distance between us today and the people of the ancient world: There are two members of the congregation at odds with each other; and there is the ever-present need for some in the church to make others a priority and to stop thinking only of themselves. The hymn about Christ is one of the most majestic passages in the entire Bible, and its main point in Philippians is that we are to have the same servant attitude that Christ did.

These things are far more easily said than done. How many churches have you been a part of where everyone was truly "of the same mind" (Phil. 2:2 NRSV)? How many families are of this sort? How many denominational leaders? How many Christian colleges? Somehow we have a tendency to bicker far more over the details than to focus on our common mind and will in Christ.

Most of us in the West do not face the pressures Paul mentioned in every one of his letters. Most of us do not really know the "sharing of [Christ's] sufferings" (Phil. 3:10 NRSV). And yet, how few of us rejoice as Paul did in this letter? How many of us have learned to be content regardless of our circumstances? How many of us truly believe we can do all things through the strengthening of Christ?

We are also prone to misread Philippians 3:12–14 as being about our current imperfection and our need to forget our past failures and to keep pushing forward to get better. Certainly these are things we should do as well, but what Paul forgot was not only his past moral failures but also his past human accomplishments. It was not a blameless life he had not yet attained—he felt quite comfortable telling the Philippians to follow his example (3:17) and expected them to be "pure and blameless" when Christ comes (1:10).

What he had not yet been guaranteed was the resurrection, the heavenly call, salvation. This is the goal and the prize, and it is for this result he urged the Philippians to live worthy lives and work together so they all make it to the end. It may be faith alone that initially secures our right standing with God, but God has given us his Holy Spirit thereafter to make us into the kind of people he planned for us to be in the first place. It is only if we are faithful through that power that we will attain to the resurrection of the dead, according to Paul.

FOR FURTHER REFLECTION

1. To what extent do you think it is possible for a church to be of one spirit or for the people in a church to have the same servant attitude as Christ did both in emptying himself of his heavenly privileges and in humbling himself to be crucified on a cross? What are the obstacles that stand in the way? What are some concrete steps you might take to become of one mind with others in your church?

2. How would you say your congregation "works out" salvation together? What are some ways you help each other live lives worthy of the gospel? Are you more likely to be faithful to the end because of the encouragement of the believers around you?

3. To what extent would you say you rejoice in both times of blessing and times of struggle? To what extent do you think you have learned the secret of being content no matter your circumstances? Can you think of others in your church that could use some encouragement? What are some concrete ways you can reach out to them and help them rejoice this week?

4. Are there any issues in Philippians that scholars discuss that spark your interest for further investigation? Anything that troubles or even angers you? Do a little extra research on that topic. Seek out another believer who has wisdom. Express your thoughts and feelings to him or her and reflect together, praying for God's guidance in your thinking and living.

RECONCILIATION AND DISAPPOINTMENT

It is not known for sure whether Paul wrote Galatians or Philippians from Ephesus. But it is pretty certain that Paul wrote at least three letters to Corinth while he was there (he also made a visit to the city that Acts does not mention; see 2 Cor. 2:1; 13:1). Perhaps surprisingly, only one of these three letters has survived for certain: 1 Corinthians. Paul's first letter to Corinth urged the Corinthians to stay away from sexually immoral influences (1 Cor. 5:9), but this letter has not survived.[1] Paul's second letter is thus the one now called "First" Corinthians.

Interestingly, the third letter Paul sent to Corinth was not 2 Corinthians.[2] It was a harsh letter—one Paul, in hindsight, was not so sure he should have sent (2 Cor. 7:8). Perhaps that is why it was not preserved. The story goes something like the following. First Corinthians tells us that there were some in the Corinthian church who questioned Paul's authority. Apparently, the conflict between Paul and these individuals led him to send an ultimatum, which he sent with Titus (2 Cor. 2:9; 7:13).

Whether Paul wrote this letter before his possible imprisonment at Ephesus or while he was imprisoned is unknown. The stark attitude of Galatians fits the apparent tone of the harsh letter to Corinth more than the mellow attitude of Paul's imprisonment in Philippians. Second Corinthians 1–9 fits more with the tone of Philippians as well. So, it appears that Paul wrote Galatians at some point after this harsh letter to Corinth, sending it with Titus.

LEAVING EPHESUS

Then there was the crisis with Demetrius the silversmith—the man who brought Paul up on charges. Paul was imprisoned. When news reached the Philippians, they sent one of their overseers, Epaphroditus, with material support. Paul wrote his letter to the Philippians, expressing his intention to come visit them. I wonder if Paul's punishment was to be banished from the city and if such a verdict might have been part of the reason he avoided Ephesus his next time through the area (see Acts 20:16–17).[3]

Perhaps Paul had intended to go directly from Ephesus to Corinth (2 Cor. 1:16). He decided instead to go to Macedonia first, which some at Corinth apparently made an issue of, claiming Paul was not a man of his word (2 Cor. 1:18–19). His desire to see the Philippians, especially after their support of him in prison, might also have played into his change of plans (Phil. 2:24).

The individual at Corinth questioning Paul's authority apparently submitted, as did the entire community—at least on the surface (2 Cor. 2:5–11). The community disciplined the person in question, so much so that Paul even told them to relax in their punishment (2 Cor. 2:6–8). Some have suggested it might have been the man who was sleeping with his step-mother in 1 Corinthians 5. There, Paul told them to hand this person over to Satan (1 Cor. 5:5) and not to eat with him (5:11).

We cannot know for certain whether this was the man in question, but he apparently submitted to the community, and the community to Paul. From this incident comes one of the most memorable verses on repentance in the Bible: "Godly grief produces a repentance that leads to salvation and brings no regret" (2 Cor. 7:10 NRSV). While Paul was not certain he had done the right thing at first, giving the church an ultimatum in relationship to his authority, his letter seemed to work and, for the moment, he was glad he did it (7:8–9). As we will see, however, it is not clear the community's submission was as complete as Paul thought it to be.

RECONCILIATION

Paul seemed to have breathed a sigh of relief upon hearing that the Corinthians had submitted to his authority (2 Cor. 1–7). The thanksgiving section (3:1–11) uses some variation of the word *comfort* ten times in this short space. It is no surprise that 2 Corinthians has some of the most encouraging words in Paul's letters.

Whether or not you accept an Ephesian imprisonment, Paul clearly left Ephesus with a strong sense of hardship and oppression (see 2 Cor. 1:8). We do not hear the resolute Paul of Galatians in 2 Corinthians, but a Paul who had been second guessing himself. His language became very polarized between the circumstances of his outer body and what is true of his inner spirit: "We have this treasure in clay jars, so that it may be made clear that this extraordinary power belongs to God and does not come from us" (4:7 NRSV).

The verses that immediately follow are some of the most uplifting in the Bible:

> We are afflicted in every way, but not crushed; perplexed, but not driven to despair; persecuted, but not forsaken; struck down, but not destroyed; always carrying in the body the death of Jesus, so that the life of Jesus may also be made visible in our bodies. For while we live, we are always being given up to death for Jesus' sake, so that the life of Jesus may be made visible in our mortal flesh . . . So we do not lose heart. Even though our outer nature is wasting away, our inner nature is being renewed day by day. (2 Cor. 4:8–11, 16 NRSV)

Second Corinthians also has some of the most ironic language in the New Testament when Paul said, "Thanks be to God, who in Christ always leads us in triumphal procession, and through us spreads in every place the fragrance that comes from knowing him" (2:14 NRSV). The Romans led a string of those they had conquered through the streets of Rome in triumphal procession. The imagery here is thus turned on its head. Paul was being led in triumphal procession, a picture of defeat, of being conquered. Yet, his persecution in the world was a sign of God's ultimate victory and judgment of the world.

THE HOLY SPIRIT AS EARNEST

The contrast between Paul's outside and inside corresponds with the contrast between his present and future. The key to that connection is the Holy Spirit. For Paul, the presence of the Holy Spirit is the key moment in moving from death to life. The Holy Spirit is God's seal of ownership, the key indication a person belongs to God (2 Cor. 1:22; see also Rom. 8:9). The Holy Spirit is also a guarantee of a believer's coming inheritance (2 Cor. 1:22; 5:5). And because of the Holy Spirit, we "are being transformed into the same image from one degree of glory to another; for this comes from the Lord, the Spirit" (3:18 NRSV).

The word that Paul uses of the Spirit in 1:22 and 5:5 is *arrabon*, a term perhaps best captured by the notion of earnest money. Think of it this way: When people buy a house, they put down earnest money, which serves both as a guarantee they will acquire the house and as a down payment toward the purchase of that house. So also the Holy Spirit is both a guarantee of salvation and, as the old hymn puts it, a "foretaste of glory divine." When we have the Spirit, we know we are headed for salvation, and the Spirit inside us gives a sense of what the kingdom will be like.

Paul's recent crisis apparently pushed him to draw a strong contrast between our current embodiment and our spiritual identity inside. Some scholars have gone so far as to suggest that Paul's thought had developed further since writing 1 Corinthians. Although most do not agree, some scholars wonder if, in 2 Corinthians, Paul believed that Christians would receive a heavenly body immediately at death, rather than in the future at the time of the resurrection. The same shift might then apply also to Philippians 1:23, where we seem to go directly to Christ at death. First Thessalonians 4 and 1 Corinthians 15, by contrast, use imagery of sleeping until the future resurrection.

In 2 Corinthians 5, Paul talked about an "eternal . . . heavenly dwelling," ready and waiting for us if our "earthly tent" is destroyed (2 Cor. 5:1–2). Scholars generally agree that Paul was referring to our current physical bodies and our future resurrection body. For us to be found "naked" would seem to mean God has not found a person worthy of resurrection, and a person does not receive a resurrection body (5:3). As in Philippians, to be away from the body is to be "at home with the Lord" (2 Cor. 5:8).

It is difficult to know whether Paul's thought had developed here or not. Most Christians assume that we go to heaven immediately at death in some sort of spiritual form. But this has not been the historic position of Christianity nor is it Paul's position in 1 Corinthians or 1 Thessalonians. In these letters, our resurrection body must wait until Christ's return. Historic Christianity has also affirmed we are still conscious between our death and resurrection. These are thus the best positions for us to adopt, even if the biblical texts at times are ambiguous.

THE FINAL JUDGMENT

Another statement Paul made that is troubling for some is in 2 Corinthians 5:10: "For all of us must appear before the judgment seat of Christ, so that each may receive recompense for what has been done in the body, whether good or evil" (NRSV). Paul made this comment to believers, not to unbelievers. In other words, he told believers they would have to give an account for their works, something he also implied in Romans 2:6–10. First Corinthians 3:15 also holds out the prospect some believers will be saved "as through the fire" (NRSV). Even though it is not popular to think so, Paul did believe our works play a role in our final judgment and even justification (see Rom. 2:13).

Paul's supposed reconciliation to the Corinthians reminded him of the very nature of his mission, commissioned by Christ himself. "In Christ God was reconciling the world to himself, not counting their trespasses against them, and entrusting the message of reconciliation to us" (2 Cor. 5:19 NRSV). This was the mission of God in Christ: to bring about the reconciliation of an alienated world back to himself. Christ, then, sent Paul and the other apostles in turn: "So we are ambassadors for Christ, since God is making his appeal through us; we entreat you on behalf of Christ, be reconciled to God" (5:20 NRSV).[4]

This magnificent passage then climaxes in 5:21: "For our sake he [God] made him to be sin who knew no sin, so that in him we might become the righteousness of God" (NRSV). With our Protestant eyes, this verse may look like a straightforward switch. Christ had no sin but took on our sin. In return, we, who have sin, take on Christ's righteousness.

But it is not at all clear Paul had this meaning in mind. The phrase, "the righteousness of God" (5:21) was a known concept within Judaism, found in the later chapters of Isaiah (see Isa. 51:5), certain Psalms (see Ps. 98:2), and even among the Dead Sea Scrolls. In these places, God's righteousness refers to the part of his character that leads him to reach out and save his people, even when they are sinful. It is exactly this subject that 2 Corinthians 5 discussed—God's propensity to reach out to his people and the world with the offer of reconciliation and salvation.

It is more likely in terms of Jewish background that Paul was saying that Jesus became a sin offering—had atoned for our sin—so that we might become a proof of God's righteousness (see Rom. 3:25–26).[5] As counterintuitive as this interpretation might seem, it seems the most likely reading when we read these words in their ancient Jewish historical context. It is thus hard to find a clear passage that says we assume Jesus' moral righteousness or goodness, despite the popularity of this idea.[6] There are passages where he functions as a sacrifice (see Rom. 3:25; 8:3). Certainly we are pronounced righteous or innocent by God on the basis of Christ. But nowhere does Paul or any New Testament author clearly say that God ascribes to us Christ's moral righteousness. This view is based on a very legalistic sense of God as a judge that seems to find little real basis in the biblical text.

MINISTRY OF RECONCILIATION

This ministry of reconciliation, to which Christ called Paul, to which God called Christ, is a ministry of the "new covenant" (2 Cor. 3:6).

The old covenant was what God made with Israel through Moses. It had a glory, but it was a fading glory (3:7). Paul allegorically reinterpreted the veil on Moses' face to signify the glory was fading. Moses' veil kept Israel from seeing the glory of the old covenant fade (3:13).

But the glory of the new covenant in Christ does not need such a veil. The glory of the Spirit of the new covenant is unfading but in fact is ever increasing in glory (3:18). And it is for this glory the people of the new covenant are destined, regardless of any current troubles or persecutions.

FRAGMENTS OF OTHER LETTERS?

The material covered in 2 Corinthians is diverse, so much so that various scholars have suggested it is actually portions of up to five different letters that have been spliced together. For example, 6:14—7:1 seems so out of place in the flow of the letter, some scholars have suggested it might be an excerpt from Paul's lost, first letter to the Corinthians on sexual immorality. These verses say not to be sexually intimate with unbelievers, and we know the lost letter had some material on not associating with sexually immoral people.[7] It is an interesting thought, but not one that can be confirmed one way or another.

Some scholars also suggest that 1 Corinthians 8–9 might have come from two different letters as well. It is true that they deal with a completely different topic than 2 Corinthians 1–7, namely, the collection Paul was receiving to take to Jerusalem. But 2 Corinthians also covers numerous topics as well. Second Corinthians 8 flows very naturally from the earlier chapters. It seems Paul was in Macedonia as he wrote, north of Greece (8:1), which is where he wrote the earlier chapters from as well (see 7:5). Second Corinthians 9:2 also fits well with Paul writing from Macedonia.

The key to understanding 2 Corinthians 8–9 is to recognize that Paul was about to send Titus back to Corinth again (8:17), even though he recently arrived in Macedonia from there (7:5–6). Two other "brothers" were also going with Titus (8:18, 22), individuals the Corinthians apparently knew, but whom Paul strangely did not mention by name. One explanation may be that one or more of these individuals stood in some way at the center of some controversy between Paul and the Corinthians.

The first is possibly one of the individuals who were with Paul in Macedonia: Timothy, Erastus, Sopater, Aristarchus, Secundus, Gaius, Tychicus, Trophimus, and—maybe—Luke, assuming he is part of the "we" that pops up occasionally in Acts (Acts 19:22; 20:4). Since the purpose of the trip was to keep the Corinthians from being embarrassed in relation to the collection (2 Cor. 9:3–4), and since the others on the list all represent other regions, Erastus may have been one of these two brothers.

Probably the best alternative for the second (8:22) is Timothy. Paul had apparently sent Timothy to the Corinthians before (1 Cor. 4:17), and it is at least possible that as Paul's representative, he had been directly involved in some of the conflict. Perhaps the reason Paul sent Titus with the harsh letter was because Timothy had become, to some extent, *persona non grata* with them. Acts 20:4 also mentions Timothy as part of the company that accompanied Paul to Jerusalem.[8] It thus seems very likely that Timothy was the one who accompanied Titus to Corinth to try to secure their portion of the Jerusalem collection.

This collection seems to have been a sore spot with the Corinthians. They expressed their desire to contribute a year earlier (2 Cor. 8:10; 9:5), but the intervening conflict with Paul derailed that process. It would be nice to think that after the Corinthians submitted, especially given the tone of 1 Corinthians 1–7, everything was back on track between Paul and the Corinthians. Unfortunately, it was evidently not the case.

Beginning in 2 Corinthians 10, there is a significant change in tone from the earlier chapters. While 2 Corinthians 1–7 include some of the most uplifting material in the Bible, Paul suddenly went on the defensive in chapter 10. Some scholars have even suggested chapters 10–13 are actually an excerpt from the earlier, lost, harsh letter. But 2 Corinthians 12:18 speaks of Titus having already returned from a visit, which places this material after the harsh letter, after Titus's initial visit to Corinth on Paul's behalf.

Some scholars have thus suggested that Paul was addressing a different segment of the congregation, a part that had not yet submitted to him, unlike his audience in the first seven chapters. The problem with this suggestion is that Paul gave no clue that he was switching audiences. There is the same word, *you*, used continuously throughout. There is simply no basis in the text of 2 Corinthians to justify a switch to whom Paul was addressing.

These last four chapters (2 Cor. 10–13) operate on different assumptions than the first nine chapters. In the first part of 2 Corinthians, it is assumed that the insubordinate individual in the congregation has repented and submitted (see 2:5–11). As we have seen, the first half expresses the relief Paul felt at his reconciliation with the community. But in 12:20–21, Paul expressed deep concerns that he would not find them as they ought to be when he came. He was afraid he would find many who had sinned earlier now unrepentant. He feared he would find the same problems he tried to address when he wrote 1 Corinthians.

Paul was not mentally unstable, so, readers face two basic options: First, perhaps Paul received new information before he sent the first part of the letter with Titus and the other two brothers. If so, however, there is the question of why Paul did not go back and revise the first part of the letter. What is more likely is the second option that— 2 Corinthians 10–13 is actually an excerpt from a subsequent letter, which was tacked on to the end of the earlier letter when they began to circulate between the churches. Second Corinthians 12:18 mentions that Paul had not only sent Titus before, but also another brother.

Thus, it would make sense if Paul sent 2 Corinthians 1–9 with Titus and perhaps Erastus and Timothy. But the solicitation of the collection apparently did not go well, and evidently, they found that the Corinthians had not submitted nearly as much to Paul as he had thought. Paul wrote a follow-up letter, which included chapters 10–13. The tone is not like Galatians. The tone is one of discouragement and sarcasm.

Paul defended himself once more, giving us another great autobiographical passage to add to Galatians 1–2 and Philippians 3. The Corinthians were apparently denigrating Paul in comparison to other "super-apostles" (2 Cor. 11:5). Perhaps they were comparing Paul to Apollos again, especially since they mentioned Paul's lack of rhetorical skill (10:10; 11:6). But the general tenor of Paul's comments sounds like his criticisms of Judaizers elsewhere.

Whoever they were, Paul called them "false apostles" (2 Cor. 11:13). Like Satan, they disguised themselves as angels of light. Paul sarcastically said he was too weak to push them around and slap them in the face (11:20), like these super-apostles. They were so wise they took pride in fools (11:19).

Paul went on to catalog the kinds of things he had endured for the sake of the gospel, things these dainty super-apostles had not faced. He spoke of how many times he had been flogged and beaten by both Jews and non-Jews (11:23–25). He spoke of the kinds of revelations God had granted him (12:1–4). Although he seemed to be referring to a different person, Paul went on to talk about God keeping Paul humble in 12:7 in a way that revealed he had been talking about himself. God allowed him to live with a physical problem, perhaps difficulty with eye sight (see Gal. 4:15), so that Christ's strength would be shown in Paul's weakness (2 Cor. 12:9).

Paul's last letter to the Corinthians ends on a somber note. He had trouble with the Galatians. He had perhaps been imprisoned and banished from Ephesus. The Corinthians remained in rebellion to his authority, unmentioned among those who accompanied Paul to Jerusalem (Acts 20:4). Presumably, they did not contribute to the collection. Paul's polite greeting from Gaius in Romans 16:23 carries great pathos, as do his words in Romans 15:23: There is "no further place for me in these regions" (NRSV). So, he looked toward Rome and Spain beyond.

LIFE REFLECTIONS

Second Corinthians is one of the hidden treasures of the New Testament. This book is full of tremendously helpful and enriching wisdom. It is easy to rejoice when things are going well or when we at least feel empowered. The Paul of Galatians is strong and forceful. The Paul of Philippians is still strong, even though imprisoned. Little can be done to change his situation, so, he rested in God. He was content. By God's power, he chose not to be anxious.

VULNERABILITY

But 2 Corinthians is somewhere in between. The first seven chapters show readers Paul at his most vulnerable. The usually confident and decisive apostle reveals the uncertainty he felt after a tough leadership decision. In chapters 10–13, he reasserts his authority but with a different tone than found in Galatians or the lost, harsh letter. Paul, here, seems less confident that the force of his personality would win the day again. He had followed God's will, fought the good fight, and could do no more.

Paul became reflective. Indeed, 2 Corinthians is probably the most reflective of all Paul's writings. It wears the scars of suffering and then of unresolved conflict. One of the best passages to read when you or someone you know is discouraged is 2 Corinthians 4:7–11. It reassures us that the way things look on the outside, the things we are experiencing in our bodies and in the world, are not the end of the story. They should not reflect what we are on the inside or where we are headed eternally. Why? Because "this slight momentary affliction is preparing us for an eternal weight of glory beyond all measure, because we look not at what can be seen but at what cannot be seen; for what can be seen is temporary, but what cannot be seen is eternal" (2 Cor. 4:17–18 NRSV).

COMMUNITY

Paul reminded the Corinthians that people do not endure such suffering alone. In fact, we are joined with the sufferings of Christ as we suffer. We are "carrying in the body the death of Jesus" (4:10 NRSV). We are joining in the fellowship of Christ's sufferings (see Phil. 3:10). And like Christ, we expect "that the life of Jesus may also be made visible in our bodies" (2 Cor. 4:10 NRSV). As Jesus trusted in God to raise him from the dead (see Heb. 5:8), so also Paul trusted to be raised from the dead (4:14).

COMFORTER

Second Corinthians also gives us incredibly rich statements about Christ and the Holy Spirit. In keeping with New Testament thinking elsewhere, Paul implied that the Holy Spirit is our guarantee of eternity, while also a foretaste of the glory already at work inside us, transforming us into the image of Christ (1:22; 5:5). If you do not have the Holy Spirit, you have no basis in Paul to say you are truly a Christian or destined for salvation on the day Christ returns.

TRINITY

Christ is God's agent of reconciliation in the world (5:19), the one who took on its sin as a sacrifice with the result that we are all examples of God's righteousness and mercy toward his creation (5:21). Paul's closing words foreshadowed full Christian belief in the Trinity and have been used for centuries to close Christian worship in the Anglican Church: "May the grace of the Lord Jesus Christ, and the love of God, and the fellowship of the Holy Spirit be with you all" (13:14). Each one of us in Christ is an instance of God's new creation (5:17) and a foreshadowing of what is yet to come.

GIVING

Finally, 2 Corinthians gives readers some rare insight into giving in the early church. There is no evidence the early Christians followed any practice of tithing, of giving 10 percent of their harvest to the temple. Spelling out what tithing was in ancient Israel highlights how different our practice of tithing is today from the Old Testament practice. Tithing was about giving of one's harvest not of one's income, as if the ancients had salaries or functioned primarily on the basis of money. Jews who were scattered in the cities of the ancient world did not tithe. What they did was pay a half-shekel tax to the Jerusalem temple each year.

There was thus no established pattern for tithing among Jews scattered throughout the cities of the ancient Mediterranean. The practice found in the New Testament was therefore less precise than commonly thought. Paul told the Corinthians they had a responsibility to support materially those who ministered to them spiritually (1 Cor. 9:4–12). Paul raised a collection to take to Jerusalem to show the solidarity of his churches with them. But none of these practices was quantified or regimented, although Paul did tell both the Corinthians and the Galatians, "On the first day of every week, each of you is to put aside and save whatever extra you earn, so that collections need not be taken when I come" (1 Cor. 16:2 NRSV).

Paul seemed to lay out somewhat of a general principle in 2 Corinthians 8:14–15:

[Y]our abundance at the present time should supply their need, so that their abundance may supply your need, that there may be fairness. As it is written, "Whoever gathered much had nothing left over, and whoever gathered little had no lack." (ESV)

In other words, all of their possessions not only belonged to God (see 1 Cor. 10:26), but they were also under obligation to give their abundance to others in the Christian community who had need. Paul said, "all who believed were together and had all things in common. And they were selling their possessions and belongings and distributing the proceeds to all, as any had need" (Acts 2:44–45 ESV).

The model for such selfless giving is Jesus Christ himself. "For you know the generous act of our Lord Jesus Christ, that though he was rich, yet for your sakes he became poor, so that by his poverty you might become rich" (2 Cor. 8:9 NRSV). This is 2 Corinthians' version of the Philippian hymn, "who, though he was in the form of God, did not regard equality with God as something to be exploited, but emptied himself, taking the form of a slave" (Phil. 2:6–7 NRSV). Paul reminded the Corinthians of the attitude they were to have toward others. After all, "God loves a cheerful giver" (2 Cor. 9:7).

FOR FURTHER REFLECTION

1. Have you ever felt beaten down by life and your circumstances? How did your situation compare to Paul's? Do you think his words in 2 Corinthians would give you hope or comfort in such times of discouragement?

2. Have you ever made a difficult decision to confront someone you believed was not living the way he or she should? How did it turn out? In hindsight, did you feel you made the right decision? How would you evaluate your motives?

3. What do you make of Paul's teaching that we who believe will also face Christ's judgment, perhaps even some punishment or reward when we appear before Christ? What do you make of Paul's hopes that the Philippians and others would be found blameless at the point of Christ's return? What do you plan to do about it?

4. How do you react to the idea that a letter like 2 Corinthians might actually be more than one of Paul's letter connected as some scholars believe? How would you fit together the inspiration of Scripture with the human processes by which it came together? Ask someone whose wisdom and knowledge you respect for his or her thoughts.

5. What is your theology of giving? Do you regularly give of your harvest to God (tithe)? Do you think Paul's letters raise the stakes by expecting believers to potentially give all of their abundance above what they need to live? Are you a cheerful giver?

NOTES

CHAPTER 1

1. As we move through Paul's life and letters, I will suggest books one might read to master Paul. Here, let me mention: Bruce J. Malina and Jerome H. Neyrey, *Portraits of Paul: An Archaeology of Ancient Personality* (Louisville: Westminster John Knox, 1996).

2. Philo of Alexandria had come to the emperor Caligula in the aftermath of a persecution against the Jews in A.D. 38. The story is found in his treatise, *Embassy to Gaius*, 352–367.

3. See, for example, Martin Luther "On the Jews and Their Lives" in *Luther's Works*, vol. 47 (Minneapolis, Minn.: Fortress, 1971).

4. Readers only learn Paul is from Tarsus in Acts, but we have no reason to question this claim. Some scholars have questioned whether Acts was overstating things to call Paul a Roman citizen. The question of whether Jews were citizens was one of the things Philo brought as an issue to the emperor Caligula (see note 2 above).

CHAPTER 2

1. Paul himself was from Tarsus in the Diaspora, was fluent in Greek, and, as often as not, quoted Scripture from the Greek translation, even when it differed somewhat from the Hebrew.

2. In Acts 23:6, Paul identified himself in the present tense as a Pharisee to the Jewish ruling council, the Sanhedrin, almost thirty years after he believed in Jesus. It was acceptable for historians of the day to compose such speeches, so we cannot be completely sure that Paul said exactly these words. But even if he did, he was surely saying it for rhetorical effect. The position Paul took in writings like Galatians and Romans is light years away from anything a card-carrying Pharisee would say.

3. In chapter 1, note 1, I began the list of books one might read to master Paul's writings. One of the best places to start the quest to master Paul, other than his own writings, is the late Krister Stendahl's, "Paul and the Introspective Conscience of the West," in *Paul among Jews and Gentiles* (Minneapolis, Minn.: Augsberg Fortress, 1976), 78–96.

Perhaps the most significant book on Paul written in the twentieth century is E. P. Sanders, *Paul and Palestinian Judaism: A Comparison of Patterns of Religion* (Minneapolis, Minn.: Fortress Press, 1977). Whether you completely agree with Sanders or not, he definitively shows that Judaism as a whole was not a religion that believed you could earn a right relationship with God. His painstaking run through Jewish literature shows that Jews at the time of Christ saw God's favor overwhelmingly as a matter of his grace and something they did not deserve.

4. The only real candidate for this argument is 1 Timothy 1:16, which calls Paul the "worst of sinners" before he believed. But as I will show in the companion volume to this book, *Paul—Soldier of Peace*, 1 Timothy differs enough from Paul's earlier letters that one should not use it as the starting place for understanding any aspect of Paul or his writings. In any case, calling oneself the worst at some point in the past can actually serve as a badge of honor in the present, as anyone knows who grew up listening to conversion testimonies.

5. One well known treatment of Paul before he believed in Christ is Martin Hengel, *The Pre-Christian Paul*, trans. J. Bowden (London: SCM Press, 1991).

6. It is the nature of tradition to make connections of this sort, to take what little is known of the past and connect it. So scholars might try to connect a Clement in Philippians 4 with a Clement of Rome fifty years later, simply because of how few Clements are know of in the ancient world. In the end, however, there simply is not sufficient evidence to know whether Gamaliel was truly the grandson of Hillel or not (or whether this is the same Clement).

7. An excellent treatment of these issues is N. T. Wright, *The New Testament and the People of God* (Minneapolis, Minn.: Augsburg Fortress, 1992), 181–203. Another book to read on a path to master Paul is N. T. Wright, *What Saint Paul Really Said: Was Paul of Tarsus the Real Founder of Christianity?* (Grand Rapids, Mich.: Eerdmans, 1997).

8. Some scholars have suggested Paul was actually a member of the Sanhedrin, given his comment in Acts 26:10 that he cast his vote against early Christians. If so, he would have had to be married and at least as old as Jesus. Perhaps it is safer to take this language figuratively.

9. I already mentioned Krister Stendahl in note 3 and referenced his book, *Paul among Jews and Gentiles*, to begin to master the study of Paul. In this book, Stendahl famously questions whether it is appropriate to use the word *conversion* at all in relation to what happened to Paul. Stendahl prefers to think of Paul's experience as a calling rather than a conversion, mainly because Paul did not change religions when he believed in Christ.

Stendahl was more right than wrong in terms of how people popularly think of Acts 9. Paul was not changing religions like we would say of someone today converting from Judaism to Christianity. Paul did not see himself changing religions, but rather changing his understanding of the Jewish Scriptures and how God planned to move forward with his people. At the same time, if we can resist using the word *conversion* anachronistically, Paul did radically change in his understanding of the Jewish faith. He turned from one sect with a distinct understanding to a quite different sect within Judaism. In that sense, we can still use the word *conversion* if we are clear about what we mean.

We must also keep in mind that we are not reading Paul's personal account of his conversion to Christ in Acts. It would have been quite acceptable for the author of Acts to tell the story of Paul's conversion in a somewhat dramatized way, perhaps even with some novelistic features. If we look at how differently the gospels sometimes tell the story of Jesus from each other, it is hard not to conclude their versions of Acts would differ just as much from Acts, if they had written them. Thus, scrupulous historical reconstruction, if we wish to do it, must always take into account the perspectives and tendencies of each source rather than assuming we are reading an account verbatim or a documentary-style presentation.

10. Richard V. Peace, *Conversion in the New Testament: Paul and the Twelve* (Grand Rapids, Mich.: Eerdmans, 1999), 25–27.

11. Remembering, however, that from the standpoint of Luke-Acts, the disciples could not properly be converted until the day of Pentecost, because it was only then that Christ sent the Holy Spirit. In Luke-Acts, as well as John, Christ's death and resurrection had to precede this event (see

Luke 3:16; John 16:7). In that sense, the lead up of the disciples to their conversion in Luke-Acts was seemingly longer than Paul's, but the conversion itself is portrayed as a moment in time, just as much as his.

CHAPTER 3

1. Paul's letters were also arguing for things, which is something to keep in mind as well—that they also present things from another perspective.

2. Two books that explore these early years of Paul's Christian life are Rainer Riesner, *Paul's Early Period*, trans. Douglas W. Scott (Grand Rapids, Mich.: Eerdmans, 1997); and Martin Hengel and Anna Maria Schwemer, *Paul Between Damascus and Antioch* (Louisville: Westminster John Knox, 1997).

3. Some, particularly Seyoon Kim, *The Origins of Paul's Gospel* (Grand Rapids, Mich.: Eerdmans, 1982), have argued that this story is Paul's version of his conversion experience. It is possible that the number fourteen is a somewhat approximate term. But since 2 Corinthians probably dates from the second half of the A.D. 50s, "fourteen years" would be about ten years off. So, while the possibility is enticing, there is no good basis for equating the two, if Acts' presentation of these years is taken at face value.

4. The classic work on the chronology of Paul is Paul Jewett, *A Chronology of Paul's Life* (Minneapolis, Minn.: Fortress Press, 1979), although Jewett's reconstruction has significant idiosyncrasies. Another work on the subject, with similar idiosyncrasies, is Gerd Ludemann, John Knox, and F. Stanley Jones, *Paul, Apostle to the Gentiles: Studies in Chronology* (Minneapolis, Minn.: Fortress Press, 1984). The main idiosyncrasy of these books is they have Paul in Greece about ten years before Acts does.

One of the difficulties with the dates and numbers Paul's letters and Acts give us is that ancients seem to have counted parts of years as years in such reckonings. Even beyond this factor, they may have approximated at times or rounded off to somewhat symbolic numbers (thus fourteen is two times the perfect number seven). So three years could be more like two and a bit, and fourteen years could be more like thirteen and a bit or even less (or more, perhaps).

5. F. F. Bruce, *Paul: Apostle of the Heart Set Free* (Grand Rapids, Mich.: Eerdmans, 1997, 2000) is the best place to access Bruce's reconstruction. Although I differ with Bruce at many points, his book is an excellent place to begin the study of Paul and so deserves an early slot among the books one might read to master Paul and his writings. Aside

from Acts, Bruce gives a very readable overview of Paul's life and writings, despite his debatable conclusions.

6. Ibid., 178–83.

7. Note, for example, Paul never mentions the letter of Acts 15, even though it was highly pertinent to some of the issues he faced in his churches. First Corinthians 8–10 addresses food offered to idols, a key item in the letter. On the other hand, Paul's omission may simply come from the fact that he disagreed with the letter, which is quite likely.

8. Bruce, *Paul*, 183–87.

9. Jerusalem was not even mentioned explicitly. Paul landed at Caesarea and went to visit the church before returning to Antioch and going again through Galatia and Phrygia.

10. It is hard to know what to do with the subtitle, Simon the Zealot (Luke 6:15; Acts 1:13).

CHAPTER 4

1. This dating works whether you think this event was more like a private visit as in Galatians 2, a public Jerusalem Council as in Acts 15, or something in between the two.

2. The scenario of 1 Thessalonians 3 is in minor tension with the account in Acts 17. In Acts 17:15, Paul went to Athens from Berea alone, and both Silas and Timothy stayed in Berea. Then Paul continued to Corinth still alone from Athens (18:5). But in 1 Thessalonians, Paul, Silas, and Timothy have all gone to Athens, and it is from there that Timothy alone returned to Thessalonica.

3. The best starting resource here, and one that deserves to be on our list of top twenty books to master Paul's writings, is George A. Kennedy, *New Testament Interpretation through Rhetorical Criticism* (Chapel Hill, N.C.: University of North Carolina Press, 1984). This book presents the categories of ancient rhetoric as someone like the author of Luke-Acts or Hebrews would have likely studied it. It is less certain Paul would have formally studied rhetoric, although it is not impossible.

4. Perhaps the best current book to understand what ancient letters looked like and what role secretaries played in writing letters is, E. Randolph Richards, *Paul and First-Century Letter Writing: Secretaries, Composition and Collection* (Downers Grove, Ill.: InterVarsity Press, 2004). Another resource is Jerome Murphy-O'Connor, *Paul the Letter-Writer* (Collegeville, Minn.: Liturgical Press, 1995).

5. D. James Kennedy, *Evangelism Explosion*, 4th ed. (Carol Stream: Ill.: Tyndale House, 1996), 73.

6. Perhaps we get at what Paul is saying better by calling it an "animal" body (1 Cor. 15:44, my translation).

7. Interestingly, 2 Maccabees—possibly a Pharisaic document—may not picture a general resurrection, but only a resurrection of martyred and unpunished wicked.

8. F. F. Bruce, for example, that great British evangelical of the twentieth century, accepted such a change in *Paul: Apostle of the Heart Set Free* (Grand Rapids, Mich.: Eerdmans, 2000), 309–313.

9. Although he possibly makes things a little more tidy than they really were, an excellent introduction to this entire topic is N. T. Wright, *Surprised by Hope: Rethinking Heaven, the Resurrection, and the Mission of the Church* (San Francisco: HarperOne, 2008).

10. This is a common idea we hear in Plato's writings. See, for example, Plato, *Cratylus*, 400.

11. From the Apostle's Creed.

CHAPTER 5

1. When it comes to this sort of analysis of the names and social status of individuals at Corinth, I should mention the pioneering work of Wayne A. Meeks, *The First Urban Christians: The Social World of the Apostle Paul*, 2nd ed. (New Haven, Conn.: Yale University Press, 2003), another book one might read to master Paul's writings. It has recently been reassessed by Todd D. Still and David G. Horrell, eds., *After the First Urban Christians: The Social-Scientific Study of Pauline Christianity Twenty-Five Years Later* (Edinburgh: T & T Clark, 2009). Another updated classic book in this area is Gerd Theissen, *The Social Setting of Pauline Christianity: Essays on Corinth*, ed. John Scheutz (Eugene, Ore.: Wipf & Stock, 2004).

2. I always struggle to know what to call these early believers. I will sometimes call them Christians, but this term often allows us to smuggle in our sense of a Christian as a religion separate from Judaism. Acts sometimes calls them "followers of the Way," but this term may very well have applied to Essenes as well, such as Apollos and the non-Christian followers of John the Baptist that Paul finds at Ephesus in Acts 18–19. Here, I use the non-biblical phrase "Jesus-followers," by which I mean individuals who believed that Jesus was the Jewish Messiah, who were baptized in his name, and who were presumed to have received the Holy Spirit.

3. We hear about this conflict from the Roman historian Suetonius (*Claudius* 25). He said the arguments were over Chrestus, a misspelling of Christus, but most scholars conclude it probably is referring to Jesus Christ. It is not clear whether all the Jews of the city were expelled or only Christian Jews like Priscilla and Aquila.

4. Roman citizens had three names: a *praenomen*, a *nomen*, and a *cognomen*. For example, if Paul's grandfather received citizenship from Julius

Caesar, he would have received his praenomen and nomen from him. Paul's full name would thus be Gaius Julius Saulus or Gaius Julius Paulus. In this case, Erastus' full name might be Gaius Titius Justus.

5. In Galatians 4:13, Paul uses a word for "first time" that may imply he had visited Galatia more than once by the time he wrote this letter.

6. This role-reversal of sorts is significant in the overwhelmingly male-oriented ancient world.

7. In the Dead Sea Scrolls document called the Community Rule, VIII.

8. The similarities between the Essenes and the earliest Christians included: an emphasis on following the Way of the Lord; the practice of sharing their possessions (as in Acts 2:44); a similar focus on specific messianic Scriptures; the apparent use of 1 Enoch (a book the Essenes seem to have considered Scripture) in 1 and 2 Peter and Jude; a common belief in the apparent celibacy of John the Baptist; a common indictment of the temple; a spiritualization of their own communities as temple communities; and a common apocalyptic outlook in terms of angels, demons, and a coming conflict with Rome.

There were also significant differences, not the least was Jesus' inclusion of sinners and apparent disregard for Sabbath and purity matters. In these regards, Paul seems more in continuity with Jesus than Jesus' own brother, James, who later became leader of the Jerusalem church.

9. Acts certainly gives us the impression that the conflict with the Roman proconsul Gallio did not lead to the departure of Paul, Priscilla, and Aquila from Corinth (see Acts 18:18). However, some scholars argue that Acts has a tendency to soften conflicts between Christians and the powers that be. But any speculation that Gallio forced Paul, Priscilla, and Aquila to leave town prematurely is exactly that—speculation.

10. It is unknown where Paul was when he sent the letter, but since Paul sent 1 Corinthians while at Ephesus, it is the best guess.

11. Some scholars have suggested 2 Corinthians 6:14—7:1 might be a displaced excerpt of the letter since it seems out of place where it is currently in 2 Corinthians.

12. The classic text here is Pliny the Younger, writing in the early second century A.D. He complains to his host for having a different menu for each person around the table based on their social status (*Letters* 2.6).

13. We should not think it impossible that there were Gentile believers who might have considered Peter more authoritative than Paul.

14. The question of Jew and Greek does not map exactly to the question of ethnicity or tribe. After all, the Jews actually were God's chosen people in a way that no other nation was. But despite their place of honor in the kingdom, Paul did deny them any greater ultimate value, status, or righteousness in the kingdom. In that sense, the question of ethnicity does relate.

15. Some people in the church are more Christlike than others, and there is a better than average chance that most people in the church could tell you who is in each category. We are not supposed to stay just as sinful in our behavior after God forgives us as we were before. There are concrete observations that, as in Paul's day, immediately indicate a person is not spiritual. But a truly spiritual person would not trumpet or boast about being so.

16. In the second volume of this book, *Paul—Soldier of Peace*, I will address the Prison and Pastoral Epistles. In general, it is argued that while some of the later books of the New Testament do follow the practices of the day in assigning different roles in the home based on gender, this is not the trajectory of God's kingdom. It does not make sense for us to maintain the roles indicative of a fallen world when it is possible for us to move closer to the kingdom.

CHAPTER 6

1. The NIV translation is quite misleading in 1 Corinthians 7:1: "Now for the matters you wrote about: It is good for a man not to marry." Paul did not concede to the Corinthians it is good for a man not to marry, but rather it is not good for a man to "touch a woman" (NRSV) in this case, a wife.

2. It is possible Jesus told wives not to separate from their husbands. Some scholars suggest that Mark 10:11–12 is filling out Jesus' teaching against men divorcing their wives for a broader context where women actually could legally divorce their husbands.

3. Here again, the NIV misses the sense in its translation: "Are you married? Do not seek a divorce. Are you unmarried? Do not look for a wife, But if you do marry, you have not sinned; and if a virgin marries, she has not sinned." Another translation reads, "Are you bound to a wife? Do not seek to be free. Are you free from a wife? Do not seek a wife. But if you marry, you do not sin, and if a virgin marries, she does not sin" (7:27–28 NRSV).

4. Jude 7 may also have to do with homosexual sex, although the phrase, "went after strange flesh" (NASB) could also mean sex with angels.

5. First Timothy 3:2 does say that an overseer in a church should be the husband of only one wife. But, in the light of what is known of the early church, it probably means one wife in your entire life, not one wife at a time. Thus, 1 Timothy expresses frustration at widows who promise they will not remarry and then do (5:9–12). (This is one of the most remarkable shifts between Paul's earlier writings and 1 Timothy, given that Paul recommends widows not remarry in 1 Corinthians 7:39–40. It is one of several reasons why a significant number of scholars wonder whether Paul was still alive when

1 Timothy was written.) So, 1 Timothy 3:2 probably means to say that the overseer of a church, whether widowed or divorced, must only have had one wife in his entire life. This instruction, like so much of 1 Timothy (such as, its teaching on women and widows), seems locked in its ancient context to where it may not clearly apply to Christians today.

CHAPTER 7

1. If, today, we have our R.I.P. ("Rest in Peace" or "Requiescat in pace"); a common, ancient tombstone was "I was not. I was. I am not. I care not."

2. Scholars debate whether the Greek word Paul used should be translated as "food offered to an idol," "food sacrificed to an idol," or "meat sacrificed to an idol." Although the debate would surely cover any food offered to a pagan god, it seems pretty clear the fundamental point at issue is meat that had been sacrificed (see, for example, 1 Cor. 8:12).

3. Remember that they would not have distinguished Christian faith from Jewish faith at this time.

4. *Lord* was a term that could be used of pagan gods as well. In the late, first century (A.D. 90s), the Roman emperor Domitian put the phrase "Lord and God" on his coins.

5. Paul takes what we might call a "nominalist" position, one that fits well with current trends in sociology and philosophy. The meaning and significance of an act (or of language itself) is inextricably linked with the context. The food itself is morally neutral. It is the context of eating, or what eaters are thinking while they eat, that makes something good or evil.

We can no doubt debate this point. Although Paul took this position on food, he might not have on some other issues. He was not, after all, presenting a systematic philosophy or theology. His thinking itself related intimately to the situations and contexts he was addressing. Many of the conflicts between Christian groups over doctrine and practice have in fact resulted from our systematizations of Paul's thought.

6. Interestingly, assuming that Matthew used Mark as we now have it (the majority position of scholars), Matthew chose not to keep this parenthetical comment, possibly implying he and his audience at least had significant doubts whether all foods were clean for Christian Jews (Matthew's audience). Mark's audience, on the other hand, was likely made up of Gentile Christians.

7. Paul may have had other motivations for avoiding such patronage. Ancient patronage came with informal expectations, with strings attached. Paul therefore may have avoided such patronage so he could freely exercise authority over his churches. The classic work here, and one we include

in the books one should read to master Paul, is Bengt Holmberg, *Paul and Power: The Structure of Authority in the Primitive Church as Reflected in the Pauline Epistles* (Philadelphia: Fortress Press, 1980). A more extensive treatment is John K. Chow, *Patronage and Power: A Study of Social Networks in Corinth* (Sheffield, England: JSOT Press, 1992).

8. This is unlike Romans 16:3 and, assuming Paul was the literal author, 2 Timothy 4:19. Acts also mentions Priscilla first two times (18:18, 26) and Aquila first only when it first introduces the couple in 18:2.

9. The other two most common interpretations are: (1) Paul was addressing a particularly showy hair style, or (2) he was not addressing a particular conflict at all but suggesting in general a woman should have long hair.

10. *Joseph and Aseneth* 5.1–2. Another relevant passage is in Philo, *On the Special Laws* 3.56.

11. In the West, we find it hard to imagine that men might be unduly tempted by a woman's uncovered hair, but a Christian from the Middle East would probably immediately appreciate this notion.

12. Some scholars have suggested the words of Galatians 3:28 might have been spoken over those undergoing baptism in the early church in some circles.

13. Aristotle's, *Politics* 1.1259a-b.

14. Jude explicitly quotes the book of 1 Enoch, which tells the stories of (fallen) angels having sex with human women. The proximity of the 1 Enoch quote to this mention of angels from the days of Noah held in chains till the judgment makes it almost certain Jude, 2 Peter, not to mention 1 Peter 3:19–20 are referring to this type of occurrence.

15. First Timothy seems to suggest that because Eve was deceived rather than Adam, wives should not teach their husbands. Nevertheless, women can be saved from the state of transgression left by Eve through childbearing (1 Tim. 2:15), a strange statement since we believe Christ atoned for all sin, including the sin of Eve. In general, it is the only verse in the Bible that forbids wives to teach their husbands (I would argue it is not even about women in general but the husband-wife relationship) and a strange one at that—not the kind of foundation one would want to base an entire theology of women or women in ministry on.

16. Verse 14:1 does not actually have the word *gifts*. It simply says, "spiritual [matters]." However, the content of chapters 12–14 makes it clear that spiritual gifts are primarily in mind, especially tongues and prophecy.

17. Some scholars used to reference 1 Corinthians 13:8 as an indication that tongues would cease as a gift, but that is clearly not what the verse is saying. It is simply saying that languages come and go over time.

18. It is hard to know when to date the Testament of Job, but it depicts the daughters of Job speaking in angelic tongues. That portion of the book may be influenced by Christians, but if it was part of the non-Christian Jewish part of the book, then it is an indication that some non-Christian Jews spoke in tongues.

CHAPTER 8

1. F. F. Bruce, *Paul: Apostle of the Heart Set Free* (Grand Rapids, Mich.: Eerdmans, 1977), 173–87.

2. Ibid.

3. That Paul was infuriated when he wrote Galatians should not be in doubt given his comment that he would be quite pleased if these individuals bent on circumcision would just "emasculate themselves" (Gal. 5:12).

4. This is an odd list of fundamental requirements for Gentiles. Many scholars have connected it to the basic expectation God had of Noah after the flood (see Gen. 9:4). The idea here is that God required of Gentiles what he required of Noah, while he expected of Jews what he required of Moses. Again, an ingenious suggestion, although I favor the interpretation that sees these four prohibitions as a solution to the question of how Jew and Gentile believers could eat together, rather than one of basic ethical requirements for Gentiles.

5. Bruce, 151–152.

6. The most notorious example is Harold Lindsell's suggestion in *The Battle for the Bible* (Grand Rapids, Mich.: Zondervan, 1976) that Peter might have denied Jesus six times: three before a first crowing and three more before a second crowing (174–176). He applied his ingenuity and created a scenario that differs more from each gospel text than each of them actually differ from each other.

7. Here, let me add to the list of books that are key to understanding Paul: the masterful collection of essays by James D. G. Dunn, *The New Perspective on Paul* (Grand Rapids, Mich.: Eerdmans, 2005). A foundational piece to read here, even though it is quite scholarly, is his groundbreaking article, "The New Perspective on Paul" (99–120). An earlier essay, "The Incident at Antioch" is extremely helpful in relation to the blowup between Paul and Peter at Antioch (in Dunn's *Jesus, Paul, and the Law* [Louisville: Westminster John Knox], 129–182). Dunn takes the second scenario position on Galatians, that it was written in the early 50s from Corinth to southern Galatia.

8. Even though I call them "missionaries of a sort," I am not insistent that the main reason these people went to Galatia was to further instruct Paul's converts. These missionaries are just as likely to have come into the area on other business.

9. It is all too easy to make this question of what constitutes right standing with God into a highly individualistic matter, something N. T. Wright has pushed back in seeing justification being just as much about being included in God's covenant with Israel as about our not guilty verdict before God. See his *Justification: God's Plan and Paul's Vision* (Downers Grove, Ill.: InterVarsity Press Academic, 2009). I would make a distinction from Wright: Incorporation into God's people is associated with justification but is not part of what the word *justification* meant for Paul.

10. Dunn, "Works of the Law and the Curse of the Law," *The New Perspective on Paul*, 121–140.

11. The document is called "Some of the Works of the Law" or 4QMMT. It can be found in *The Complete Dead Sea Scrolls in English*, rev. ed., trans. Geza Vermes (New York, N.Y.: Penguin, 2004), 221–229.

12. The expression is "the faith of Jesus Christ." To understand the debate, you have to look at a phrase like "love of God." What does this phrase mean? Is it God's love, as in "The love of God led him to send his Son"? Or is it our love for God, as in "Your love of God should lead you to serve him better"? The phrase Paul used, "faith of Jesus," could also mean either the faithfulness of Jesus or faith in Jesus.

Yet another book to add to the list of resources is Richard B. Hays, *The Faith of Jesus Christ: the Narrative Substructure of Galatians 3:1—4:11* (Grand Rapids, Mich.: Eerdmans, 2002). I only partially agree with Hays, but I also only partially agree with the notorious response of James Dunn, reprinted in the back of Dunn's book (249–271).

The three main reasons I finally concluded that the first expression in Galatians 2:16 and Romans 3:22 refer to the faithfulness of Jesus are: (1) the redundancy of that would be created by Galatians 2:16 referring to faith in Christ three times in the same sentence; (2) the parallelism with Romans 5:19—"through the obedience of the one man the many will be made righteous"; and (3) the notion of faith in 2 Corinthians 4:13—while the train of thought is hard to follow, this verse seems to say that just as Jesus had faith and was resurrected, so we must also have faith and be resurrected, thus substantiating that Jesus' faith was one of Paul's categories. However, I also agree with Dunn that Paul goes on in the majority of instances after Galatians 2:16 and Romans 3:22 to refer to faith directed toward God.

13. It is significant to point out that a Jew, indeed Paul himself, would not have categorized things this way.

14. Thus E. P. Sanders' famous line, keeping the Law for Jews was about "staying in" not "getting in," *Paul and Palestinian Judaism*, 17, 420.

15. The Lutheran World Federation and the Roman Catholic Church, *The Joint Declaration on the Doctrine of Justification* (Grand Rapids, Mich.: Eerdmans, 2000).

16. The only place this expression is found is in James, which says a person is not justified by faith alone (James 2:24).

17. E. P. Sanders put it this way: Paul "thought 'backwards' from the revealed solution—that God sent Christ to save the world—to the plight from which he saved it—that all things were 'under sin.'" *Paul* (Oxford: Oxford University, 1991), 41. There are many other overviews of Paul on the market today (like this one), each of which gives its own spin.

CHAPTER 9

1. This order has nothing to do with the order in which they were written but with their length. The earliest nearly complete manuscript of Paul's writings has them ordered from longest to shortest, with Hebrews second.

2. The same can be said of Philemon, where Paul tells Philemon to prepare a guest room for him (Philem. 22). If the book of Philemon was written from Rome, it would also imply a significant change of trajectory for Paul.

3. Remember that Jesus was taken to the "praetorium" of Pilate in Jerusalem (Mark 15:16); the same word used in Mark 15:16 is used in Philippians 1:13.

4. A quick comparison of Luke 24 with Acts 1, which covers the same period, would also lead to the same conclusion.

5. Paul addressed this point to his "loyal companion" (NRSV) or "loyal yokefellow." Some scholars have suggested the word *yokefellow* is actually this man's name, Syzygos. But I think Paul is likely referring to Epaphroditus, who probably was the one who delivered the letter of Philippians back to Philippi.

6. Another book to read to master Paul's writing is Ralph P. Martin, *A Hymn of Christ: Philippians 2:5–11 in Recent Interpretation & in the Setting of Early Christian Worship* (Downers Grove, Ill.: InterVarsity Press, 1997). While not an easy read, Martin explores the main options for the interpretation of the Philippian hymn that scholars have suggested over the years.

7. N. T. Wright has argued this point. One of his early books was a collection of articles (*The Climax of the Covenant: Christ and the Law in Pauline Theology* [Edinburgh: T & T Clark, 1993]), which includes articles on key texts about Christ like these verses from Philippians. Whether you agree with him or not, I think this is one to read to master Paul's writings.

8. There are some notable exceptions. For example, James D. G. Dunn is perhaps the best-known proponent of the idea that the first line is actually about Christ being the second Adam who undid the fall (*Christology in the Making: A New Testament Inquiry Into the Origins of the Doctrine of the Incarnation*, 2nd ed. [Grand Rapids, Mich.: Eerdmans, 2003], 114–121). Adam was also in the "image of God" (Gen. 1:27), but he did grasp at equality with God. Jesus, in the same situation, did not grasp in that way. Dunn thus did not see any indication of Christ's pre-existence in the hymn, since it was as a human on earth that Jesus did not take advantage of being in the image of God. Most scholars, however, have not followed Dunn's interpretation. For example, it is not clear that "form of God" (2:6 NRSV) means the same thing as "image of God."

However, I consider it a strong possibility that "form of God," whatever else it might imply, relates to Jesus having the status of God, that is, of being God's Son (cf. Tobit 1:13). That it has to do with status is supported by the parallel phrase, "form of a slave" (2:7 NRSV). The stanza thus comes to say that while Jesus had the status of God, he did not take advantage of that status, but instead, took on the status of a servant. On this reading as well, it would not be entirely clear that Paul was referring to Jesus in some pre-existent state.

9. N. T. Wright has taken some pains to make it clear that this expression does not mean Paul was saying that we will go to heaven or spend eternity in heaven, only that heaven is where our empire is centered (*Surprised by Hope: Rethinking Heaven, the Resurrection, and the Mission of the Church* [San Francisco: HarperOne, 2008]).

CHAPTER 10

1. Some scholars have suggested that 2 Corinthians 6:14—7:1 is really a displaced fragment from Paul's first letter.

2. Again, some scholars have suggested that 2 Corinthians 10–13 might be an excerpt from Paul's third, but now lost, letter.

3. First Clement mentions that Paul was once banished (5.6). This would also contribute to the reason there was no more room for Paul to minister in the East (see Rom. 15:23).

4. The "you" in 5:20 is an interpretation rather than something in the original. Some scholars think the sense is, "We ask on behalf of God [to people in general], 'Be reconciled to God.'"

5. N. T. Wright is best known for this interpretation. A good summary of his argument appears in "On Becoming the Righteousness of God," in *1 and 2 Corinthians, Pauline Theology*, vol. 2 (Minneapolis, Minn.: Fortress Press, 1993), 200–208. This four volume series, *Pauline Theology*, is a

resource that presents the thinking of the leading experts on Paul in the 1990s.

6. N. T. Wright's positions on these sorts of things may sometimes be a little too stark (for example, he tends to resist the possibility of exceptions to generalizations of this sort). Nevertheless, his book, *Justification: God's Plan & Paul's Vision* (Downers Grove, Ill.: InterVarsity Press Academic, 2009), is where he deals most accessibly with the question of "imputed righteousness" from Christ, that is, the idea that Christ's moral righteousness is ascribed to believers in order to satisfy the justice of God in acquitting us. I do not believe Paul was this legalistic in his sense of God's justice.

7. Paul clarified in 1 Corinthians 5:9–13 that he primarily had immoral believers in mind, not unbelievers. Second Corinthians 6:14—7:1 has often been used in popular teaching to argue against dating or marrying unbelievers, although the topic of sex and marriage is not what is under discussion there.

8. Although, interestingly, Acts never mentions the collection Paul raised for Jerusalem. This curiosity has given rise to its own share of speculation among scholars.

Apply Paul's Teaching to Everyday Life

Messenger of Grace Bible Studies

The life and writings of Paul make up a large percentage of the New Testament. Yet many Christians struggle to grasp their significance because the culture and concerns they address seem so far removed from our own life experience. The Messenger of Grace Bible Study series, based on Kenneth Schenck's *Paul—Messenger of Grace*, helps small groups and individuals go deeper in their understanding of Paul and his letters.

Like the book, these studies begin with sound scholarship and focus on applying Paul's life and letters to contemporary life in a practical way.

Each six-week study focuses on one of Paul's letters from the earlier part of his ministry and includes both weekly and daily study components.

Our Joy
Philippians
Kenneth Schenck
$7.99
ISBN 9780898274424

Our Hope
1 Thessalonians
Kenneth Schenck
$7.99
ISBN 9780898274417

wesleyan publishing house

www.wesleyan.org/wph or call toll free
1.800.493.7539 M–F 8 a.m.–4:30 p.m. ET

Life Lessons from Paul's Later Letters

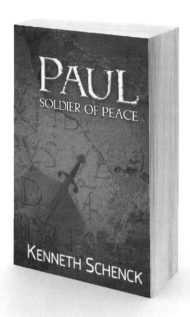

He went from persecuting the Jewish Christians to battling the principalities and powers so that he could extend their Christian faith throughout the Greco-Roman world. Author Kenneth Schenck bridges time and culture to bring you *Paul—Soldier of Peace*.

Schenck delivers more than a narrative recounting of history; each chapter concludes with the author's insightful reflections of how Paul's life and letters can shape our lives more into the image of Christ. *Paul—Soldier of Peace* covers the later part of Paul's life and ministry including Romans, Ephesians, Colossians, 2 Thessalonians, 1 and 2 Timothy, and Titus.

Paul—Soldier of Peace
Kenneth Schenck
$14.99
ISBN 9780898274400

wesleyan
publishing
house

www.wesleyan.org/wph or call toll free
1.800.493.7539 M–F 8 a.m.–4:30 p.m. ET